D1530712

float you

READY TO
YOURSELF

TAKE TO MARKET?

float you

how to capitalize on your talent

Carmel McConnell and
Mick Cope

www.yourmomentum.com
the stuff that drives you

What is momentum?

Momentum is a completely new publishing philosophy, in print and online, dedicated to giving you more of the information, inspiration and drive to enhance who you are, what you do, and how you do it.

Fusing the changing forces of work, life and technology, momentum will give you the right stuff for a brighter future and set you on the way to being all you can be.

Who needs momentum?

momentum is for people who want to make things happen in their career and their life, who want to work at something they enjoy and that's worthy of their talent and their time. momentum people have values and principles, and question who they are, what they do, and who for. Wherever they work, they want to feel proud of what they do. And they are hungry for information, stimulation, ideas and answers....

Momentum online

Visit *www.yourmomentum.com* to be part of the talent community. Here you'll find a full listing of current and future books, an archive of articles by momentum authors, sample chapters and self-assessment tools. While you're there, post your worklife questions to our momentum coaches and sign up to receive free newsletters with even more stuff to drive you.

More momentum

If you need more drive for your life, try one of these titles, all published under the momentum label:

change activist
make big things happen fast
Carmel McConnell

lead yourself
be where others will follow
Mick Cope

happy mondays
putting the pleasure back into work
Richard Reeves

the big difference
life works when you choose it
Nicola Phillips

innervation
redesign yourself for a smarter future
Guy Browning

snap, crackle or stop
change your career and create your own
destiny
Barbara Quinn

hey you you
pitch to win in an ideas economy
Will Murray

coach yourself
make real change in your lfie
Tony Grant & Jane Greene

from here to e
equip yourself for a career in the wired
economy
Lisa Khoo

grow your personal capital
what you know, who you know and how you
use it
Hilarie Owen

PEARSON EDUCATION LIMITED

Head Office
Edinburgh Gate
Harlow CM20 2JE
Tel: +44 (0)1279 623623
Fax: +44 (0)1279 431059

London Office:
128 Long Acre, London WC2E 9AN
Tel: +44 (0)20 7447 2000
Fax: +44 (0)20 7240 5771
Website: www.business-minds.com

First published in Great Britain in 2001

© Pearson Education Limited 2001

ISBN 1 843 04006 9

British Library Cataloguing in Publication Data
A CIP catalogue record for this book can be obtained from the British Library.

10 9 8 7 6 5 4 3 2 1

Typeset by Northern Phototypesetting Co. Ltd, Bolton
Printed and bound in Great Britain by Biddles Ltd, Guildford and King's Lynn

Cover design by Heat
Text design by Sue Lamble, London

The publishers' policy is to use paper manufactured from sustainable forests.

dedicated to ...

Stuart Driver
Richard Rosen

and to everyone
who dreams of
CV-free success

now float

start here

your float strategy

staying afloat

momentum

float you

opening

pages x / xi

start here

float you

momentum

float manifesto

1   This is the age of the individual – as such we all own the right to manage and exploit our personal capital for personal benefit and the good of others. The implication of this is that we are also individually responsible for what happens in our lives.

2   We believe each person has the power to float – maybe not right now – when they choose to take action and give the appropriate time to the change.

3   Float is not the answer – it is the challenge.

4   We want to float each person with joy. Our goal is to awaken a spirit of enquiry, a passion for life. To Float You in a way that is fulfilling, sustainable and rewarding.

5   Our belief is that change in behaviour is predicated by a change in language. We are consciously and overtly aspiring to change the language used in society.

6   We will never run float programmes solely for the well funded – our intention is to offer access to float technology to everyone in society.

7   We have and will continue to apply all principles in this book to ourselves. We are happy for anyone to e-mail us to talk about where we are on our float journey:

carmelmcconnell@btinternet.com
mickcope@wizoz.co.uk

momentum   float you   start here   pages 2/3

float journey

Why this book?

'I have not got a clue what my personal capital is, or what it is worth.'

Is that true for you? If so, you are not alone. This is a collective Achilles' heel, inherited from the pre-knowledge era, when we were all herded together under the category 'hired hands'. We were not meant to know our value or that we had marketable personal capital. That's changing. But there is a lot of catching up to do.

Let me give you an example: we spoke recently to a successful media industry manager, very socially skilled, with an impressive corporate track record and degrees aplenty. He phoned to talk about a potential career move. After half an hour on the phone we got onto the importance of knowing your own value. He asked, 'do you know anywhere I can find something to read on that?' And I didn't.

What are you worth? Look at your career right now, and ask that question. It is like gazing into a mirror that allows no reflection. But the mirror image is growing clearer. And a main reason is the era of global market deregulation, which has stimulated the deregulation of human capital. The age of the individualized economy is coming closer.

What is driving this? Factors include:

◆ **Access to money.** If you have access to a good idea or solid asset, financial investment is becoming less of a barrier to entry into the world market.

◆ **Growing social emphasis on self-provision.** For example, previously paternalistic governments are withdrawing pyschological comfort blankets such as state support for education and pensions.

◆ **It's not what life hands you, it's what you do with what life hands you.** The knowledge economy values results not ancestry, giving rise to greater global work opportunities for those equipped to navigate the wired marketplace.

◆ **Global mindset.** We live and work in a global electronic village.

◆ **Increased career expectations.** Each generation has accelerated the rate of gain in living standards. One extension of that has been changing attitudes to work. This generation is increasingly concerned about how to find work with meaning, how to be happy, as well as pay the bills.

What has this got to do with you? Plenty. Although most people in salaried employment will still find the concept difficult to personalize.

You can choose what you think, where you work, who to work for and when.

But to achieve this you will need to invest in your biggest asset, you. We want to help. We believe you will be happier and more in control of your life when you realize your own personal capital and that is why we have devised the Float You concept.

Where from?

Many of the ideas have evolved from our earlier work. This book offers an integrated approach to genuine, sustainable life change. We hope that where something really grabs your attention and causes you to reach for more information you can go to our other books for more detailed information on the float levels. The other books are:

◆ Lead Yourself, (Mick)

◆ Know Your Value. Value what you know, (Mick)

◆ Change Activist, (Carmel).

You can find more information on the Float You concept at our website: *www.float you.com*. You will also be able to use the float capability index to help you think through your current state of readiness to float. Or contact us directly at our personal web pages. Carmel's is *www.changeactivist.com* and Mick can be found at *www.wizoz.co.uk*.

What we aim to achieve

To help you optimize personal value in the market.

This is an achievement manual authentic to our experiences. We'll help you figure out how to make it happen in the real world. We won't guru you. We won't use bull. We'll hopefully befriend you. We won't enthuse then lose you.

If, like us, your life is still not a total success story, learn from our experience. We've screwed up, worked it out, made it happen. We will show you how to take one aspect of your life and change it consistently.

You will surface.

float you

momentum

Book structure

This book is built around the following structure:

Start here

◆ **Their change is your change** – why the time is right to Float You

◆ **Your personal capital** – outlines the broad concept of the Initial Public Offering process and how it relates to you. The key chapters are:

   – The IPO steps

   – What is float?

   – Your float potential

Your float strategy

◆ **Float levels** – introduces the 5 levels within the Float You framework:

   – Know yourself

   – Know your value

   – Know your network

   – Know your market

   – Now float

Staying afloat

◆ **Float plan** – helps you to move into the action phase by focusing on what you can do and what other resources are out there to help:

   – Planning

   – Resources

Float candidates

At first some of the concepts in this book may seem difficult to apply to your life and the changes you wish to make. To ease this journey we have included studies of three different people who might be on a similar journey to your own. Similar, but not the same, as everyone's journey is his or her own. The experiences they go through in applying Float You might help you to make the connection with changes you wish to make in your own life.

These are the three Float characters whose journey will be followed through the book:

1 **Launched Lisa** – leaves her job (she's sick of working for sad old geezers), re-trains in new technology skills and starts an internet marketing company;

2 **Muddled Martin** – works out what he wants to do and changes his role to become a force to be reckoned with right here and now with his current employer;

3 **Potential Paula** – Completes an adult literacy programme and starts a pre-university entry course. The world is her oyster but she still feels as if she's under ten feet of water.

their change is your change

Let's put the concept of economic self-determination in some context. How come most of us don't know our value? Partially because that is the way the current economic system was set up to work. Historically, only a minority had enough of anything to bother auditing assets and income with any accuracy. Land – how much? Factories – how profitable? Legal advice – for what hourly rate? Those outside that priviledged circle had little need to measure, because there was so little to measure.

But that is changing. Because of the factors detailed earlier (in Why this book?), global economic conditions have changed. As individuals we are now potentially powerful players in an evolving global strategy of pricing and resourcing, based on new rules. And as individuals we need new ways of thinking and acting if we are to prosper in this new economy. To see ourselves as financial planners within our own personal economies.

Most importantly, we'll need perspective to see ourselves as distinct individual economic units, to determine the value of our personal capital.

Let us describe our view of those new economic conditions, to help set the wider stage within which we aim to Float You.

The contemporary model of capitalism, which has emerged over the past 30 years, is young, aggressive and dynamic. We believe this is a US-based global economic system. It is characterized by global entrepreneurs, the corporate entities, which have increased in influence through access to relatively cheap, flexible capital and technology. Since the end of communism as a viable economic model, capitalism has become the global monopoly. And, paradoxically, it seeks to impose monopolistic demands on those of us allegedly most able to choose. Let us explain.

Under the now discredited Soviet economic system (1929–89), the Government collectively decided what ordinary people would need, how much people could afford to pay and then instructed centrally owned farms and factories to supply the market according to those predictions. It didn't work because central planning on such a large scale is technically impossible. And it didn't help that the system was largely corrupt.

Eventually the economic system broke down, then the political. The Berlin Wall came down and everyone was free. Which meant free to shop, if you had the cash.

Alternatively, in the blue corner, we have the market economy, using price to allocate goods in short supply, based on the unhindered actions of willing buyers and willing sellers. This is the free market system, with America as the top student in the class – doing well. The US economy represents 25 per cent of global financial activity and, as we keep hearing, when the US economy sneezes, the rest of the world catches cold.

We believe we now have a new economic hybrid, which lies somewhere between free market and command economy. Adam Smith wrote (in *The Wealth of Nations*) of an invisible hand, by which he meant that if there is perfect competition, everyone is free to choose. He stated that the outcome in this situation is optimal for everybody. Thus the market did not have a conscience, but the price mechanism acts as an invisible hand to get the best results for everybody. Now we do not suggest that the invisible hand has vanished. Just that Western governments and large corporations have consolidated a lot of market power, producing an unbalanced system. The invisible hand appears closed to some in the global economy and open to others. This creates greater economic freedom

start here

float you

momentum

for those able to engage at the most dominant, affluent levels. It restricts the activity of those with limited financial means, for example developing nations, poorer income groups and less profitable businesses.

We believe we now have a new economic hybrid, which lies somewhere between free market and command economy.

This new hybrid is, in our view, currently under-regulated. Although Adam Smith and others viewed perfect competition as a suitable substitution for conscience, we suggest that under-regulated perfect competition doesn't always produce the best outcome for everyone. For example the G7 nations were unable, at the most recent Climate Control talks, to persuade the conglomerate interests of the US to reduce carbon fuel emissions, in order to reduce global warming. It didn't suit the oil revenue lobby to cut production because that would mean less profit. As one industry sector in a monopoly hybrid, this group was able to set conditions against the wishes of democratically elected representatives. The rising tide of consumer protest is one symptom of this hybrid economy out of balance.

Float You is not intended to be an evaluation of the new world economic order (for more on that see *Banker to the Poor* by Mohammed Yunnus (Aurum Press, 1998), *No Logo* by Naomi Klein (Flamingo, 2001), *Change Activist* by Carmel McConnell (momentum, 2001) and *Business As Unusual* by Anita Roddick (Thorsons, 2000)). But we plan to help you do the best for yourself in a changing economic marketplace. If you don't want to think of yourself in economic terms, consider your social choices. Political will bows to economic will, which in turn creates our social climate. The hybrid economy impacts everyone alive and trying to earn a living today.

So consider your own situation. Do you see yourself as a confident, free economic entity?

A global market context for Float You

Soviet 'command' economy	Free market	If this is true, it is a hybrid economy	Now check with these questions
Employer allocates supply of work and price of labour (employee wages) depending on senior Government or top management decision.	Employer allocates supply of work and price paid to employee according to relative scarcity of product or service. Therefore employee salary (price) is determined by market activity.	In a command economy you are told what to do. In a free market you negotiate. In the hybrid economy you may be pointed towards a life path by circumstance, e.g. place of birth, but negotiate destiny using skills, determination and so on.	Are you in your ideal job? Did you have free choice over your current work?
Individual has limited say over income increases within the centrally regulated system.	Individual negotiation on income with potential employers based on market value of knowledge and scarcity of resource.	Income levels are defined by the marketplace. We can choose which part of the marketplace to operate in.	Did you negotiate your personal income? How?
Individual is dependent on factors outside his/her control, such as centrally defined education and social policies. These largely dictate personal income and lifestyle.	Individual is able to improve personal conditions by making choices within a relatively open education and social ladder. Bias exists but may be overcome through exceptional personal achievement.	Many people choose education based on potential for future earnings. Generally, where the individual is independent of the market, e.g. wealthy, there is scope for artistic or creative expression.	Did your education expand or reduce your career options?

Soviet 'command' economy	Free market	If this is true, it is a hybrid economy	Now check with these questions
Self improvement in material terms is unlikely.	Self improvement in material terms is likely for high-achieving individuals.	Although national wealth increases year on year, historical patterns of social deprivation remain intact.	Year on year, are you getting richer?

The market condition in which you operate has a direct bearing on your personal float success. Float perspective means evaluating the nature of your current market – at strategic level – so that you are better equipped to navigate towards success. Your float is linked to factors outside your control. So it is best to know what they are.

Float You = float more than you

The release of personal capital at individual level is good for everyone. How? It is a bit like oxygen being released into a stream. More oxygen, more fish. More fish, more everything, right the way up the food chain, all the way to you and me.

In the same way, the ability to develop skills and know-how and deploy them without fear creates a critical mass of utilized personal capital for the organization. Imagine people in your team full of ideas for improvement, adaptation and creative expression; being louder and probably more effective. Scale that up one level to your organization as a whole. In a knowledge economy companies differentiate on a number of factors. One factor is the quantity and quality of actively engaged 'intangibles' (that's you and me in accounting language, folks). If your management team has come up with four top-selling products in the past year, you can bet that adds to the value of the company. Going one more step up, creating a society full of those types of organizations must surely add to the earnings potential of 'Our Country Inc.' (*see* Fig. 3.1).

In conclusion, maybe this wish to break free of the bounds of corporate slavery and create value in partnership 'with' and not 'for' the parent company is symbolized by the Initial Public Offering (IPO) *see* page 18). Many large companies use this as a way to let a young fledgling business break free of the corporate reins and take its own chances in the market. It is this spirit of release that we have tried to embody in the Float You process. Just to re-emphasize, this is to break free from in order to create a new working relationship – not to sever the current relationship. We believe that it is in the process of moving from a reactive to a proactive and then on to an interactive relationship that new value is created for all players in the relationship.

float you

momentum

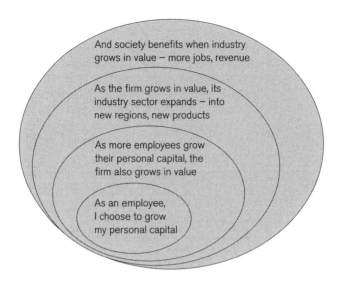

Figure 3.1 *Good for everyone*

We believe that people who build value for themselves will also create value for their employers, family or other stakeholders.

Healthier companies or families will lead to stronger economies, higher living standards and more career, personal and business opportunities for individuals. This is a loop of abundance where we all can win.

the Initial Public Offering (IPO)

Throughout this book we have you in mind. We are going to help you define and structure your success based on well-established financial principles of market flotation. So it seems worthwhile to take a little time here and now to simplify the IPO process. Just so you know.

The float process

One IPO story: Larry's Lorries

Age 18, Larry borrowed £200 to buy an old van. He used it as an extra resource for a home removal business. He worked evenings, weekends, and over a year saved enough for a new van. Then another. Then two more. He and his wife came up with their own 'LL' logo, and lovingly had it painted on every van.

Now age 38 Larry has a home removals business of his own with 22 vans and drivers. He also diversified into food logistics and now sub-contracts another 15 refrigerated lorries to a frozen foods firm. Although the firm turns over a lot of revenue, it is hard to get enough profit to achieve Larry's lifelong dream of being a global logistics player, with Larry's Lorries doing business first in Europe, then America, one day even Australia. Larry loved the idea of lorries carrying his 'LL' logo whizzing through the Australian outback, bringing frozen food to the most remote communities.

But to grow the business in this way he would need big investment money. He would have to borrow almost half the value of his business. Rather than take out a huge loan, the family and board of directors decide to raise cash by selling 40 per cent of the equity in their company, in the form of shares.

They appoint bankers and slowly get through the stringent tests necessary to become a publicly listed company. Then they talk to potential investors. A price per share is agreed by the financiers, based on factors such as Larry's track record, potential for growth in the new marketplace and the credibility of his management team. Fund managers think Larry is a reasonably sure bet and will want to add shares in his company to their stock portfolio.

The big day comes when shares are issued publicly (the Initial Public Offering or IPO). 1,400,000 shares are offered at $2 and go up to $2.5 in one day. This brings in $3.5 million. Larry has the money to buy his next set of lorries and achieve his dream. Larry's Lorries has floated.

This chapter looks at the IPO process – considering the route taken by lots of firms just like Larry's Lorries.

Capital is the lifeblood of trade. You need cash to start a business and cash to grow a business.

When a firm has established a business model with a good level of profit, it becomes possible to offer equity in the company through shares. Most companies need to raise capital in stages. Early on, money is needed to create the prototype product or service. In these early years of growth, funds are typically provided by venture capitalists (VCs) or other forms of private investment. This is known as private capital investment. (NB Larry didn't need this as he grew the firm funded by sales.)

As the business grows it develops a bigger appetite for capital, used, for example, to fund new product development or build brand awareness. So the float process moves on, with the company seeking larger amounts of investor money by appealing to the public markets. The first time this happens is termed the Initial Public Offering (IPO).

start here

float you

momentum

Why go through all this? Well simply because it is extremely hard to run the business, pay suppliers, employee salaries and produce more product funded solely on day-to-day revenue. An extra $50 million will make your business move along at a faster pace. Giving better returns, faster, with improved financial opportunities. For the owners, personal value increases with the firm's market success. For investors, fast return gives the chance of fast re-investment. The IPO is therefore validation, proving that you have successfully cornered an area of the market with something people want to buy. Because you have done that, all being well, investors will want a part of the action – the underlying assumption being that your firm will return a profit that will give a healthy dividend payment on their investment.

Given that this is going to apply to you in a minute, let's take a closer look at the stages which make up a complete float. Here is one venture capitalist manager's view of the float process.

1   Business idea.

2   Develop prototype product/service and market test. Prove business model.

3   Produce business case and seek venture capital meetings. Pitch. Win funding from private venture capitalists.

4   Keep proving the business model by adding brand recognition, customers, market share. Decide to offer shares to the public markets (IPO) to access greater funds.

5   Appoint expert advisers – accountants, lawyers. Commence due diligence.

6   Produce float prospectus. Embark on investor roadshows. Market the issue to institutional shareholders and the public. Fix price based on investor feedback.

7   Issue shares – float.

8   Use cash from shares to fund growth in business operations.

The Float You process

Now let's apply that to you. There are five float levels that roughly correspond to those key steps in gaining public investment.

IPO steps	Float levels*
Business idea.	Know yourself
Develop prototype product/service and market test. Prove business model.	Know yourself
Produce business case and seek venture capital meetings. Pitch. Win funding from private venture capitalists.	Know your value
Keep proving the business model by adding brand recognition, customers, market share. Decide to offer shares to the public markets (IPO) to access greater funds.	Know your value
Appoint expert advisers – accountants, lawyers. Commence due diligence.	Know your network
Produce float prospectus. Embark on investor roadshows. Market the issue to institutional shareholders and the public. Fix price based on investor feedback	Know your market
Issue shares – float.	Now float
Use cash from shares to fund growth in business operations.	Keep going

*NB Each level includes aspects of all the other levels, because the float process is iterative. For example you will have spoken to some people (know your network) and done some market research (know your market) before writing the business case (know your value) at a very early stage.

The float team

Assembling the ring of confidence

The management team of a company seeking to float on the public markets will need to appoint a team of advisers, known as the IPO team. These must include the following:

- investment bankers
- accountants
- lawyers
- publicity team / investor relations / financial printers

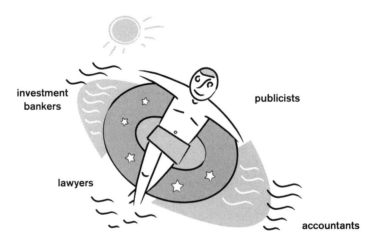

Figure 4.1 *The IPO float team, a ring of confidence*

Getting the very best advice on your side is a key part of float success.

For example the bank acting as adviser needs to have analyst coverage of the specialist marketplace in which your company operates. Which means that there will be someone helping you who really understands market conditions, pricing and likely future trends. But what if the best banker doesn't feel that you are good enough to advise? Similarly, failing to get a 'big five' accounting firm can be a real hindrance – investors will ask why, and be less confident in the offering.

Float advisers and IPO firms are in a closely knit relationship. They win win or lose lose together. Take one example. Your failure to disclose information about the past activities of your company – perhaps a little creative accounting in the early days. If the discrepancy isn't picked up by your advisers during the due diligence phase, then market damage could be huge for all parties. Some investors have even sued on claims misrepresention. This is important in two ways: first, your name gets linked to theirs – so it's critical to have experienced advisers acting for you who will add to investor confidence in the IPO. Second, you need to be successful enough and squeaky clean enough to win big financial advice for yourself.

Meanwhile, you're maybe wondering about the quality of your own float advisers. Let's examine what the market analogy has to offer at individual level.

Your personal float team

Who can you call on to help with your personal float? Who'll give you that ring of confidence?

This is not an exhaustive list – we're simply making the point that you are not going to succeed in your personal float unless you have lined up some good expert advice. And that applies whatever your circumstance, so whether you are trying to move jobs or launch the most amazing new product, consider first of all who is on your team.

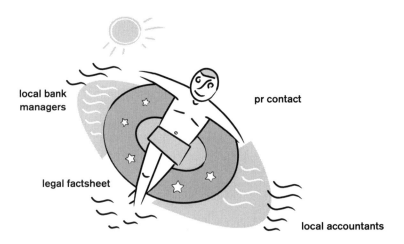

local bank managers

pr contact

legal factsheet

local accountants

Figure 4.2

Who will help you with these various activities?

- **banker** – raising funds, managing cash flow, dealing with short-term overdraft, etc.

- **lawyer** – advising on any legal factors within your float.

- **accountant** – who will make sure you optimize your cash positon and tax liabilites?

- **publicist** – helping others know that your float is about to hit the market.

Lisa's float team

Lisa's decided that she has had enough of being passed over for promotion. She has resolved to make a change. As she says, 'I am pretty fast with software, I get all the new versions installed, can do web pages and stuff! As we rejoin Lisa's float journey, she has booked herself on a web design course and decided to find out about starting a small web site design business. The question is how to assemble a float team to assess Lisa's float viability.

Float team member 1, the local accountant
Her husband Ben knows someone at the local business link office. Lisa makes a phone call to the centre and is given the number of a local accountant. They arrange a meeting. The accountant is able to help Lisa

calculate start-up costs and potential income from a web site design business.

Float team member 2, pr contact
A friend at the office used to work on a newspaper. She knows someone who is a freelance PR person. Lisa meets her for a coffee and offers to do some free web site design in return for help with the wording of a brochure. They get on – and find out that their kids go to the same school. The PR contact might even be able to get a little local press coverage, if Lisa comes up with a good angle for the local paper.

Float team member 3, the local bank manager
Lisa goes to her bank manager. He likes the fact that Lisa has savings and is working on a business plan. Agrees a back-up overdraft for six months at a reasonable interest rate. This meeting does wonders for Lisa's confidence. The bank manager also advises Lisa to start a business account and invites her to come in for a monthly chat.

No sign of a lawyer yet, but the business link gave her a basic legal factsheet on starting a business.

What does Lisa think about it all?

Lisa's update
This has been a brilliant couple of weeks. I gave my notice in at work (sing it with me, na na na, na na na, hey hey hey, goodbye!!) and I leave end of next month.

I took a long weekend and went to the local business advice centre last Friday. Ben's firm does some kind of business support for them, so he ever so politely insisted I talk to the accountant there. Anyway it was good. Her advice was not to overstretch things financially until I build up customers at a price range I can make a profit on. She was a bit worried about my lack of experience, but liked my web ideas, and the fact that I am so determined – in fact she might be able to refer some of her customers to me to maintain their web sites. Apparently lots of small companies have got web sites which they never update. So that might be where I can help.

Meeting Mr Andrews at the bank was really good as well – I was so nervous going in. There was this little voice in my head saying 'who do you think you are Lisa – don't make yourself look like an idiot'. But now I know I have the bank's support if I need to borrow a bit until the first few invoices get paid, I think I'll sleep a lot easier. And he was so nice! He said 'that's great Lisa' when I said I wanted to start my own company. Should have videoed it for my mum! So I have now got an overdraft arrangement which means six months guaranteed bills and mortgage paid. It might take a while, he said, until my first customers pay up. I hadn't thought of that but he's probably right.

Ben's noticing how different I've been … We went to the park with the kids on Monday afternoon and I went on the swings myself instead of pushing them! It's because I feel like a big kid again – so nervous and excited at the same time. Talking it through with the right people has been really good. I know it can work, listening to them.

Your float team – here and now

Now over to you. Consider your team. List as many people as you can – think of friends of friends, people in your organization.

Advice area	Names of potential float advisers
Investment / market advice	
◆ Who could help – list names	
◆ Who is best to help	
Money/financial advice	
◆ Who could help	
◆ Who is best to help	
Legal advice	
◆ Who could help	
◆ Who is best to help	
Publicity / marketing / getting your message out	
◆ Who could help	
◆ Who is best to help	

This exercise illustrates the help you have at your disposal – or the lack of it. A company about to float on the public markets needs the best specialist advice available. If you are going to make your plans a reality, so do you.

The IPO process is something that works – even through the highs and lows of market turbulence. Even if you have a fantastic idea and are completely high on newfound entrepreneurial energy, take stock of the last big stock market shift, and work out your next move.

start here

float you

momentum

Float value

How much are you worth?

Individual market value depends on our own reading of current marketplace conditions and the current value placed on similar offerings at least as much as on the intrinsic worth of the product or service being offered.

The economic theory behind a float – or any business case – contains both fact and analysis. For example, for someone working as a chef their ultimate goal could be the creation of a perfect dish, say an amazing fresh tomato and basil soup. The soup is its own reward for the chef, partly because it represents the pinnacle of professional achievement and reinforces his position as a top chef, partly because it will be named after him and give him personal pride. For the restaurant owner, it means a guaranteed income from happy soup-loving customers. So the business case for the production of the soup would have many of the same facts, but depending on the author, show vastly different analyses.

Market analysis is subjective. Market facts are objective. Generally. If this is the case, we should feel very optimistic. Because if the financial markets are fuelled by information which is supremely relative, rather than absolute, then surely deployment of the right personal tools and techniques with regard to those relative criteria will improve our marketing position?

What is your business worth?

taken from www.entrepreneur.com

Q How do I place a value on my company?

A In reality, valuing a business is much more of an art than a science. The most widely accepted value will be defined by how reasonable the figure is relative to the assumptions used in the analysis. Most financial professionals will admit there's as much qualitative input as there is quantitative number-crunching when it comes to performing valuations.

Valuation can be derived from any combination of the following eight models:

1   net assets after all debts are excluded;

2   net liquidation at fair market pricing;

3   replacement costs at existing market levels;

4   adjusted goodwill on excess earnings;

5   recent comparable sale price;

6   comparable public company price;

7   comparable price-earnings multiple;

8   present value of after-tax cash flow;

Those clever financials applied to you

Your value could be determined using some of those financial appraisal models. Let's consider (and explain) some of those tools of financial appraisal, numbers 2, 5, 6 and 7, as they may apply to you.

Net liquidation at fair market pricing:

Applied to you

What would be the total amount you would gain if all your assets were sold off? The garage sale proceeds from everything I own – even if everyone in the area had one the same day! (E.g. for a property owner, this would mean less worth because if the property market hit a time of maximum house sales, prices would be depressed.)

Recent comparable sale price:

Applied to you

What was the total financial reward when a person just like you put everything up for sale?
What your neighbour got for the biggest garage sale of his life.

float you

momentum

Comparable public company price:

Applied to you

Is there a business which offers comparable product and has a similar track record? What does the market estimate to be the value of that company? What is the share price of your nearest competitor?

Comparable price-earnings multiple:

Applied to you

The relationship between a company's share price and its after tax profit divided by the number of shares. How long will it take to get my initial investment stake back at a good rate of return?

As with any financial indicator, these are just that. An indicator, not the answer. It might be that many of the indicators shown above do not apply to the change you wish to make. However, we suggest that you do a double check just in case. So many people and companies float when things are buzzing and the feel-good factor is high but fail to really appraise their financial situation as it might apply when the down-turn hits. Make sure that you are clear on your debt, liquidity and potential return to be sure that this is a step you and your stakeholders wish to embark upon.

How much are you worth to your boss, cash?

There is a theory of economic value that suggests an item is worth less if it only has one customer. Monotony? No that's not it. The opposite to monopoly, monopsony. That's the one. The crucial thing about monopoly / monopsony is this: Under perfect competition, each agent has no control over his prices. They are the market prices and they are given to each competitor. A monopolist or monopsonist can set the price of a product for which he is the only supplier or the only customer.

Example 1 Monopoly
The Royal Mail in the UK can choose how much to charge for a stamp. If you would rather not pay the 26p, too bad. This is a monopoly imposed by law.

Example 2 Monopsony
Junior doctors in the UK can only work for the NHS, there being very few private hospitals. In the US doctors are able to earn large salaries because hospitals compete to hire the best doctors in the free

marketplace of unregulated healthcare. Likewise, before privatization train drivers could only work for British Rail. This monopsony means that a lower wage level is set, and at this lower wage fewer people are willing to work.

Going back to that well-known economic theory of market dominance and family *bored*game (anyone else had to babysit pre-teen entrepreneurs?), with a market monopoly in place there is one producer and lots of buyers. With a market monopsony there is one buyer. Therefore there is some economic theory in support of our Float You contention that your labour is worth less if you sell to a single buyer. You improve your salary if you are able to sell to multiple buyers. Question for you. Do you sell your labour to a perfect competition marketplace, a monopoly or monopsony? What are the implications of each?

Let's look at Lisa. In perfect competition she cannot set the fees for her web design work. In a monopoly Lisa's is the only web design firm in town so she is able to set high prices. In a monopsony Lisa has just one customer, who is likely to pay a lower rate for the work.

Take a moment to jot down your own current situation.

Your income is set for you by perfect competition.* Changes depending on market conditions.	You are in a monopoly and can set prices in the marketplace.	You are in a monopsony with one buyer and accept their prices.
Evidence yes	Evidence yes	Evidence yes
Evidence no	Evidence no	Evidence no
Is this good or bad for your ability to optimize personal capital?	Good or bad?	Good or bad?

* NB: One important assumption about perfect competition is perfect information — where there is a market price, it is given to everybody and we all know what it is. For example everyone in the organization knows everyone else's salary. In reality this assumption is rarely met, because we all operate in slightly different markets. Your market is people who do your job, and within that job there are even smaller niche markets such as people who do your job with two years' experience, or five years' experience.

How did you get on? Did thinking about your life in that way seem a bit odd? The purpose here is to define and assess yourself as an economic being. It isn't easy and it might feel a bit clinical or harsh. We know. It isn't very comforting to know that your labour and my labour is a commodity, to be traded more or less like potatoes. Which is why Float You thinking is so crucial. Our goal is to help you realize your true worth and that means some pretty thick scales dropping away from your eyes. And heart.

Here is another question. How do you know if your labour is fairly valued? What is the value to the firm of you turning up and doing what you do? That's easy. Your salary. Or is it your salary plus car plus pension, plus gym membership, plus 10 per cent if you say you have another job to go to? We are woefully low on information about the profit or loss your firm realizes on your contribution. What, less costs, do you do for the bottom line of the firm?

At individual level, let's look at you, the separate financial entity. What about the shares you have tucked away, the property quietly appreciating around you? What are your costs? Does your material worth improve year on year or do you find yourself slipping down the ladder of prosperity towards something too horrible to consider?

Can you calculate Gross Domestic Product as it applies to you? Do you know the elements of your personal economy and have a sense of your future economic trends? Do you have any idea of the value a financial analyst would put on you, as a person, right now? If you do, well done. You are in the minority. Here is why.

How do you shape as dealmaker for yourself?

Perspective is hard to find when it comes to career and financial well-being. So for a moment, consider yourself as a potential business, up for sale.

◆ What will you do with it?

◆ What is the product or service being offered?

◆ Would the investment be able to generate at least 10 per cent return on capital over the next five years?

Or if that isn't working for you, imagine that your current firm was being bought out. You and some of your colleagues were asked if you wanted to stay or leave. Here are some questions. Remember the purpose of these is to highlight your options – and give you a new way of looking at your financial destiny.

◆ How much money do you think you could make if half of you left the firm and advertised (ethically) a better service to current customers of your firm?

◆ Would you be better off accepting a new permanent role, with share options and some longer term security, or a higher paying contract for one year?

◆ What if the new owners gave you a chance to start a franchise – paying you $300 per day for three months, with marketing and product support, after you stump up $100,000 for the first year licence. Is that a good deal?

◆ What if someone else offered you a million now, in return for 30 per cent of your future salary, to be paid to them in cash each year until you are 60? What are the pros and cons?

◆ Would you accept $200,000 tomorrow, if offered, for the rights to your future words, brand ideas?

◆ Is anyone likely to buy?

A management team becomes 'intangible assets' (tangible assets, by the way, include the nice downtown premises bought by the same management team earlier in the year), and someone says – yep $500,000 can be added to the value of that firm because of the e-retail expertise of the guy with red hair in the front row.

The value of one individual to the firm is now a concept that has started to work its way onto the largely unprepared balance sheets of large organizations.

The highly paid specialists who help companies go through an IPO are essentially helping investors to make sense of the companies, goals and plans for the future. In the same way, this book will help you to help others make sense of your goals, plans and future ambitions.

In the next chapter we start to help you to understand the five float levels and how they will take you on your personal journey to the surface.

personal capital

Take a deep breath and get ready. Because we are going to Float You. Our goal is to help you rise from the depths, where you feel pressured, underutilized, fearful. And, take you to the surface where you are able to navigate a personal journey of your choice. In this book we will help you learn how to equate the financial event known as an IPO or, more colloquially, the float with five stages that will help take you and your worth to market. To become self propelling, steering on your values, going as fast as your human limits allow and then some.

There has never been a better time to think and act free

The idea of personal capital – the value any marketplace can put on the unique skills and potential of any individual – is a concept now ripe for exploitation. And to those of you who are open to the potential of personal capital, *this is your time* and this is your guidebook.

Your personal capital (is not London)

Do you remember the first time you got both feet off the ground in the local swimming pool, started floating, then swimming? That amazing 'rule the world' feeling you got from moving across the pool? Float You provides the framework for your decision to float, the support that means that you can take off the water wings, go deeper, go for the dream. As defined by you. Have you defined it?

Given that you wouldn't advise your best friend to jump into a deep pool if they couldn't swim, or to risk their life savings on one company share, this book aims to give some alternative investment strategies for your best asset, you. Just think about how you invest yourself in the market. Have you taken the safe route and set up a funding agreement with a single company? Have you given them you as an asset in exchange for the paycheck, pension and performance review? The problem is not in making this investment decision, but in not understanding the risks associated with this investment decision.

Imagine you are on a backpacking trip around the world, you are in a strange country and you are down to your last rouble, drachma or dollar. Someone offers you the chance to invest your money in a new venture. The upside is that it might give you enough money to get home by Christmas. The downside is that you might lose all your investment and end up working in the local McDonald's for the next two years saving up a return fare.

In this situation you are being asked to invest all your eggs in one basket and have a portfolio mix of 'one'. As such we believe you would carefully weigh up the odds of the investment, you would decide if you can trust the co-investor, understand the market, talk with friends about the problem. As a result you might invest your all in this one opportunity or you might decide to hedge your bets and invest half your assets in this venture and invest the other half somewhere else.

In the same way we are suggesting that the next time you get a job you are making an investment decision – but this time you are investing yourself as the primary asset. And in many cases people are placing themselves into a portfolio mix of 'one' – where they have taken a company job. By making this decision you have undertaken a risk – and a risk that affects you, your family and future – that the choice to work with a company or colleague is the one that will maximize the greatest return on you. Even by taking a job you are floating yourself on the market.

It is important to stress that we are not advocating that you give up company life and work for yourself. We are suggesting that any choice you make regarding who, where or how you work is an investment decision and as such you need to evaluate the value of your capital before you enter a trading arrangement with someone else in your market.

Our individual fate is tied to a greater or lesser extent to the same factors of concern to the business seeking funds for investment, such as market conditions, network, experience. So why don't we try to evaluate our potential using the same process? Some dot.coms did (ok ok, we know) but even post-bubble the lessons learned point to a new economy of branded intangibles. Human capital is increasingly starting to float free from the constraints of corporate control, free of the limits of local marketplace. Float free and move up.

When did you say?

Have you ever been indoors, working away through a perfect morning of blue skies and warm breezes. About to go out. In a minute. I'll just finish this. It won't take long. Looking up to see those blue skies grown grey. The moment gone.

The day is passing and guess what? You still plan to get out later. Float You provides experience and compassionate detachment that might help you get out, and enjoy your own blue sky. Because it might well cloud over. Life can, and for many people, does. 'Any regrets? Don't talk to me about it love, I didn't have the chances you young people have today … '

Float You asks you to consider yourself, your life, your talents as a viable venture. Worth your investment. And the first investor is you. Your time, energy. Float You wants to help you pull yourself up off that mental sofa, the one marked 'staying here until fear of rejection subsides' and get going. First of all to help you define success in your terms – which probably is more than just money. Your success in terms of love, social contribution and self-fulfilment. Being a success by your standards, living to your values.

start here

f l o a t y o u

m o m e n t u m

Your float process is halfway through

Growing up is a mini float process. We find ourselves able to choose and take risks towards even more choices. As we become more independent we create more choice. As we become able to define our priorities we find fulfilment. More independence equals more choice seems to be the pattern.

But that level of independence doesn't seem to translate in the same way in the workplace, or the area of personal capital. There are some choices that until now have been off limits. Well this is the strange bit. While our route to independence seems unstoppable during those early years, there is often a jarring halt as soon as we reach the heady heights of being an employee in our first steady job. Interview, second interview, hold tight and you're in. Regular money, somewhere to sit down that isn't in front of your parents and away you go on the road to promotion and a truly comfortable lifestyle.

We get all the way to 23 taking our own decisions then, suddenly, it's 'no sir I have no opinions save yours'. 'And your opinion is a very fine one sir, if I may say, just before my appraisal is due, without it seeming too ingratiating. Sir. ' Of course we don't hand over all our autonomy when we become employees. We lobby for rises, consult on where we sit, take action even if the parameters change completely. But generally speaking, somehow our first role in the world of employed people smacks of re-applying those nappies. Can I go to the bathroom please, during the boss's presentation? Ah. Better not.

Our contention is that you reduce the value of your personal capital by becoming the unassertive not-quite-grown-up employee, as soon as you hit the workplace. Think about your own life, right now. You have skills, hopes, expertise that certainly have value in the marketplace. Do you know – outside of the pay you get right now and the internet job ads for similar positions – your true worth in the marketplace? What would you say your true value is to the firm? Have you ever considered that your current boss could be a human asset stripper? How do you find out if your employment situation is taking an unfair margin on you? On the side of the employer, the equation still holds. Having a cowed workforce might have been ok 25 years ago, but now the psychological contract has changed and good people look for a partnership with mutual benefit. So being the most effective employer – and employee – means having a good understanding of the concept of personal capital, so that you can optimize your value in the marketplace.

Here's how. By learning to Float You. Birds do it. Bees do it. Even unknown small Venture Capitalists do it. So let's do it, let's Float You. (yes, we know, the words don't go like that, thanks anyway.)

Float You – optimize your value

We use Float You as a wider metaphor for the attainment of personal success on your terms. Float You is a process whereby you release your potential and thereby optimize your value in the market. And each one of us is different. Each one of us is just as important. Personal capital is measurable in societal and moral terms. The person who creates a local nursery and chooses to provide the best possible pre-school education has personal capital. The person without a home to look forward to has personal capital.

From learning to earning. Learning – not only in financial terms. Earning – not only in financial terms. Learning to identify our strengths, our skills, our unique spirit. Earning by fulfilling our potential – yes, getting the megabucks if that is what you want – and equally getting the megabuzz of contribution and personal satisfaction. Earning in terms of family time and balance. Earning in terms of being able to live on your own independently. Earning in terms of happiness.

Float You is the term we have given this journey. It starts from where you are now – with however much untapped, unmarketed personal capital. And it may never end in the same way as a publicly listed organization can never stop growing, evolving and adapting to the ever changing demands of the market.

Float You is the process of taking your light out from under that bushel. Bushel? Was that a biblical txt msg describing Business Hell?

Float. Because the tide just turned …

In our careers, we are evolving into two discrete species. First, those of us who want to pay a broker – let's say our present employer – some of our labour market rate. Second, those of us who want to be our own brokers, going with our personal skills, expertise and experience direct to market.

For those of us who want to trade what we do direct to market, understanding and using the concept of personal brand value and brand capital is a survival skill. For those of us who don't currently trade direct to market, understanding personal capital is still a survival skill. Why? Well, when you know your worth, you will be better placed to take advantage of the free market known as where you work. That's right. The internal organization is a free market. Think about it. No one knows what is going to happen in future. We can choose to react to stuff as it happens or choose to direct our lives.

The tide just turned and potentially you ride the wave or get stranded.

start here

float you

momentum

Join the FU2% club

This book will help if your goal is to become self-sustainingly successful – buoyant – by building a solid foundation of self-mastery. This is not a 'change-your-life-for-ever-by-deep-breathing-and-eating-raw-food' book. It doesn't predict a 100 per cent happy ending. Life isn't a quick change adventure. So there is a recognition that we all have the potential to float, but the pot of gold – venture funding – only makes its way to 2 per cent of firms who sent their business plans to investment banks, so it is reasonable to assume that many reading this book will not be able to float. At this point in time.

This is a key point in the Float You philosophy so let us say it again – as a rule of thumb – only 2 per cent of the applications for venture fund investment receive funding – in the same way only 2 per cent of you reading this book at this moment in time are ready to successfully float! If your response is to say 'I am one of the 2 per cent', then as a quick test go to three people – your bank manager, partner and friend – and ask them if they would like to financially invest in you. Look into their eyes and see if you are ready to float.

However, the caveat here is 'at this moment' in time. We believe that 100 per cent of our readers have the capability to float. The Float You model will help you get the determination, and capability to take you into the FU2% club.

Even if the thought of floating is far, far away, and your life is simply about getting from one bill to the next right now, we passionately believe that Float You thinking is going to be useful. And next spring, who knows? What can you do now? Well you can think of your future and mentally paint the picture of improvement. See the success that could be waiting for you to claim it.

Expecting your life to improve is the first stage of success.

Our float experiences

Carmel's Float

I have bought and semi-read loads of books on how to change your life, ignored loads of good advice, put the best ideas off until this afternoon, decided not to do anything until after one more cup of coffee. I planned to talk to people, to make things happen. But I just didn't. And all the things I never said became unwanted guests inside my head.

What were we saying? Oh yeah. Months later. Pick up another self-improvement book, read it avidly, take notes. Perhaps remember one or two lines. But never do anything about it.

By the time I was 28, I had been at work for 12 years, been a social activist for 7 years and truly felt the best years were over. I had nothing more to look forward to. My idea of becoming a lawyer got trampled because the inner procrastinator incarnate told me I was too old. Ok, that was a lucky escape. But generally it wasn't good.

Yet another day was spent wondering where the morning went. TV soaps became hugely important. Years passed. But somehow I did change. I just got tired of hearing the same truth and having no good answer to the increasingly persistent question, 'what are you going to do about it?'.

By this time I was 30 and being 40 was about ten minutes away. So I decided to talk, gently, with my lazy, inconsistent, weak self and come up with a deal to give my life a second chance. Falteringly. Of course I lost the first, second and third 'list of things to do to change things'. But I did keep the fourth. Float You is written from the experience I have had since that time.

These are the facts. In 1990 I earned less than £8k a year. I had lost the longest relationship of my life. I had no formal qualifications, having left university to live at the peace camp at Greenham Common. My parents died young and I had a dependent younger sister alongside. A friend said to me recently that she used to be embarrassed when people asked, 'what does Carmel do for a living?' and just say I hadn't found my niche. In fact, I refused all niche suitors because I felt I had been there, done that and didn't want to play anymore. So just leave me alone, ok? My head was not an easy place to live in.

Eleven years on. I am fine financially, I am more active in the area of social contribution than I have ever been. My sister is independent and happy and I have to work hard to get time in her diary. Home life is shared with an incredibly wise and beautiful woman and I love her with all my heart.

What changed between 1990 and now? I changed my thinking.

In my twenties my career left me ill equipped. I lived in a world of protest and campaigns (and am still proud of the achievements of the peace movement). But as I was used to being anti-everything, becoming pro-something seemed too strange. I somehow worked out that my self-image – being one lone fighter in a hostile world – was hurting me the most. I started to accept myself and others, even old foes, as just being in transition. All of us doing our best.

My inner voice – an indication of my deepest beliefs and values – started to encourage me rather than judge everyone and everything, harshly. Things started to get comfortable and I accepted offers of help. (Thank you to the fantastic generous teachers who gave me such wonderful support. You know who you are.)

I started working harder, began to study. Got my masters degree. Took more risks. Found more stimulating work. I read *Feel the Fear and Do it Anyway* by Susan Jeffers (Arrow Books, 1991). That made a big difference. As an anti-nuclear activist I did scary things (like sit down next to police horses in the traffic) to gain attention to a cause I passionately believed in. It took me ten years to figure out that being happy was a cause worthy of just as much passionate belief!

Things are easier inside my head and therefore in my working life. I am still learning how to trust. One last thing. I notice that as I value myself and honour my worth, others follow. It also works in proportion. Funny that.

Mick's Float

I scare easily. I get scared when I don't have any money. I get scared when I have too much money. I get scared when on my own and scared when I am in a roomful of people. Because I scare easily I spent most of my life running scared.

I guess my float journey is less about making money, having the latest 100hz flicker-free TV (whatever that is), or buying the latest S-type Jag. For me float is about not being scared to be me or face the world any more.

It is difficult to look back now and say when my float started. There was Peter Madder-Smith, the senior technician in BT, who helped me know where I was going and helped me go back to college to retake all the failed exams. There was Ed Percival who helped me to know my value when I decided it was time to jump ship from BT (after 24 years). There was Sara, Dave and all the rest of the group of people who helped me to understand the sheer power and joy of operating in a network. There was Paul Oliver who helped me to understand the need to know your market. And there was Carmel, who pushed me to understand and know that I was ready and that the only way to do it is to do it.

However, I think the real turning point was when I decided to leave the safety net of working for people and to make the shift to working with people. After 24 years in a large corporation, and one year in a small consultancy firm, I finally decided to branch out on my own. The fear, anxiety and worry was quite staggering. I was fortunate that I had the encouragement of my wife, Lin, and my children, who all supported the decision. But, I thought, what if it doesn't work, what if I am no good, what if the market takes a downturn, what and if what if?

Then came a point when I sat in the office, desperately trying to make the decision to leave, and I suddenly thought 'If I don't value myself, how on earth can I expect anyone else to value me?'. I stared to realize that I had to take me seriously and at that point the first lead boot was released, as I began the float journey to the surface.

For me the float journey starts and never stops. It is just an endless series of flotations, with each minor float sitting inside a major float that sits inside a meta float. Like the bubbles rising to the top of the ocean, you rarely see just one bubble, instead you just see a seam of action where pockets of air are moving from a lower point to a higher point, and that is enough to know that flotation is occurring.

start here

float you

momentum

Lisa's float

I don't think I've done too bad. Didn't have a clue about what I wanted to do, so I left school, got an office job and qualified as a secretary at night school. I earned reasonable money, had a lot of fun. Party years really. I met my husband when I was 22 and was able to work flexible hours after our sons were born six years ago.

It was just that it has got to the point when I have *just had it* with doing everything apart from going to the bathroom for my latest boss. I arrange her shopping, cover for her to her boss when she can't be bothered to finish reports – everything – and still no chance of my name going forward for the junior management job in marketing. 'Don't you think you'd be unhappy with all that extra responsibility?' I thought, 'Listen, honey, I run this place so don't even go there – ok?' But I just smiled. It isn't worth fighting when they've made their mind up about me already. Especially her.

I suppose that conversation was a bit of a turning point. Because after about three years of thinking about it, I have now decided to get myself away from being someone's office servant and become someone who one day will have a secretary of her own. Ben (my husband) is a bit worried about how we'll manage if I leave this job – his firm isn't as financially solid as it used to be. But he really wants me to be happy and tells me I am smarter than the whole senior team put together anyway. And the boys are at school now. So – providing I can find work with about the same pay within three months we can manage on our savings until then.

I have got to do something. The trouble is deciding what. I am pretty fast with software, I get all the new versions installed, can do web pages and stuff. Maybe that – or am I too old? Internet jobs go to bright and shiny college kids don't they? Anyway the boom is over. And I am 28. Not exactly a spring chicken. Are we sure we don't want another baby? The twins are getting so grown up. A girl would be nice. Uh oh, oh no. Thinking pressure overload! Where is all this going to lead? At least I know the ropes here. Or it is that I know how to allow myself to be boxed onto the ropes here? Have I got a big change in me? Seems to be I can't stay here, and I don't know where else to go right now. HELP!!

Your float

Think about your journey so far and try to answer the following questions:

your passport photo

◆ On a scale of 1 to 10, how successful do you feel you are right now?

◆ How would you describe your life journey so far?

◆ Who has helped you make transitions and major changes?

◆ What have been the points in your life where you have taken small floats − changing your life for the better?

◆ Who helped you with those mini floats?

◆ What floats have you attempted that didn't work?

◆ What would be your float dream?

◆ What is your personal capital and what is its value?

◆ Where are you now?

It is a big deal that you have started to think about your float journey. What was it like? Have you thought about this before? Could you describe it to a friend?

What we hope to do is to help you think about structure and ultimately present your float in a way that others can understand and invest in. The key is baby steps, consistent and regularly taken towards where you want to go. Your thinking isn't going to do it. Your action is.

It is easier to act your way to a new way of thinking than it is to think your way to a new way of acting.

Marianne Williamson, *A Return to Love*, Harper Collins, 1996

start here

float you

momentum

your float strategy

float five levels

The Float You framework is a simple but powerful structure to help you determine if you are in the 2 per cent of people who are ready to float now, and, if not, what action you might take to get there. It doesn't give all the answers, but it does ask you the right questions. We both wish we'd had the framework when we started our floats!

The framework is influenced by two key factors. First, the generic IPO model that drives a commercial business float and, second, a wealth of shared experience and learning as we have gained a better level of control over our lives. It is important to stress the word 'influenced'. In the same way that there is no single commercial float model, there is no single process for floating an individual. However, in the same way that any commercial float will have generic steps, any personal float will have a number of factors – shown in the picture on the next page.

Float-U

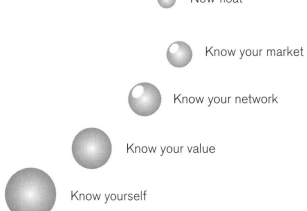

Now float

Know your market

Know your network

Know your value

Know yourself

Figure 6.1 *Float levels*

We believe that the following five levels, in this sequence, will greatly aid the Float You journey:

◆ **Level 1 Know yourself.** Only 2 per cent of people who say they want to float are ready *at that moment in time*. At this stage of the float model you really start to find out about yourself and your capacity to act.

◆ **Level 2 Know your value.** How can you become absolutely clear on the value you are taking to market and the value others will place on it? You will assess whether your float value is a niche offering or a commodity, and how to place a market value on your float offering. Apart from your assets, what liabilities do you have that counteract your value; and what return do you expect on yourself as an investment?

◆ **Level 3 Know your network.** Personal capital is just that – it is the value that you have, own and are able to take to market. You can have a scarcity mentality about it, treating it as something to hide and hoard. But if you do that, your personal capital will never grow. If you develop an abundance mentality, however, and allow your capital to socialize with other people's capital, there is a chance that you can create social capital with enhanced value. The

float you

momentum

network multiplier effect. Networking is nothing new. When Gandhi started his personal journey the first steps were made by development of a coalition of people with shared interest. He understood that by mobilizing the power of his network he could take his ideas to market and help enhance and realize their value. You too can learn how to build and manage your network to maximize your float value.

◆ **Level 4 Know your market.** There is little point in floating yourself as the best producer of mobile phones in town if the world has changed and everyone now wants to buy a combined mobile phone/personal digital assistant. There is little point in becoming the firm's expert in Australian online buying habits if the new owner has decided to focus on the European market this year.

◆ **Level 5 Now float.** The final stage is action. You will become an activist for the cause of you. How can you make it happen? By creating a campaign plan with your float as the campaign goal. The only way to do it is to do it. You start feeling better after you take action. The secret is in practical steps, each one potentially a new and important personal achievement. Each one will build courage and confidence. This is where it all happens.

your float strategy

float you

momentum

level 1
know yourself

First of all, let us paint a bleak little picture. Failure to really know yourself can lead to a personal flotation that is painful, costly and potentially damning to yourself and those you care for. If you don't give yourself time to understand what really moves and motivates you, the whole process could be built on a castle of sand. However, build a solid layer of self-awareness and self-confidence and become sure of your journey.

The flip side doesn't bear thinking about. Those budding rock stars who find they hate being on stage. The fantastic artists numbed by a blank canvas, who find they just can't find any inspiration (sadly some weeks after ditching the day job). Entrepreneurs who gamble house and home on a whim and lose everything. There is the potential to leap into the brave new world only to find that it is more of a dark abyss than a welcoming bright light of opportunity. The investment in knowing yourself (reasonably) means big payback further down the road. And, like all big projects, the cost of change gets higher the further down the track you get.

Signpost

So here we go. As you start to lead yourself through this stage of the float process, there are a number of important decisions to be taken. These decisions are singled out to help you think about the 'you' in Float You. To raise questions about your commitment, focus, decision criteria, relationships and a host of aspects that might seem trivial at the moment but will cause your float to come tumbling down at a later date if not thought through.

The six points in this section cause you to think in more detail about yourself. If you want to climb inside this level any more, please look at the book *Lead Yourself* written by Mick (momentum, 2001). This will help you understand the key factors that drive how you will lead yourself through the whole float process.

◆ **Choose your choice.** Although you might believe that you manage choice in your life, the reality is that we often concede or trade away much of this power to others. Effective flotation is dependent upon the extent to which you regain the freedom to make choices, and then create choice muscle to continue making choices.

◆ **Know where you're going.** There is little point in harnessing the power to manage a personal flotation unless you know where you're going. Somewhere fabulous, somewhere worth working for. A peach of a beach. At home with all the toys fired on bluetooth. A lover's dream come true. No less. To get there, first stage is to define a set of clear personal goals and outcomes to use as criteria to guide the flotation. Think of each one of those goals as a progress marker. They will help.

◆ **Map your map.** The choices you take within the float processes are driven by your ability to create a fantasy that guides your float. The bit that makes it happen will be grounding the adventure in facts, data, feedback.

◆ **Change how you change.** Embark on this float process and it will be fundamental. You will change more than a part of yourself. You are making a significant and lasting shift to the way you think, feel and behave. To achieve a float that is successful and sustainable, you need to figure out how make changes across all five levels of the change ladder (coming right up.)

◆ **Step inside out.** Your personal success needs to be defined within your world. Built on understanding what success is for other people in your circle of transformation, as well as yourself. Think of the people in your life as investors in your transformation. Your actions may impact their lives, so it makes sense to work out what is in it for them, early on. That's right. Understand the potential changes to people who will be close during Float You. To do this it is important to step outside of your view of the world and into theirs. See success from their perspective – draw up a list of the three you most care about. When you understand how others think, feel and behave you can truly understand what success looks like for them. Call it mutual benefit, enlightened self interest or simple courtesy – this is critical to your success.

◆ **Share success.** Here's a big one. Personal flotation that is selfish, exploitative and low on respect is going to be short lived. And that is not true success. An authentic float is founded on shared outcomes, social responsibility and sustainable success. And we can prove it.

Six decisions. As you take control of these six decisions, you enhance your ability to Float You properly and, more importantly, significantly reduce the risk of problem or failure downstream.

Choose your choice

So, you say, I have made my choice – I want to float myself and release my potential. Well, that might be your choice, but is it your choice to make?

Ignoring – for the purpose of sanity – the many social and cultural factors impacting how much choice we have. Let's say you begin life with some choice, but then feel that you have no choice but to trade some of it away in exchange for life's creature comforts. In the small boat of our lives we steer – or we don't steer – depending on what, exactly? Is it fair to say we can move the rudder according to our degree of choice?

Who really controls your rudder? To what extent do you have control? Who else might be steering? Did they wrest it from your grasp, or did you hand control over voluntarily?

Consider the following questions:

- Who chooses when you have a beer?
- Who chooses what shoes you wear?
- Who chooses where and when you work?
- Who chooses your income?
- Who chooses when you get promoted?
- Who chooses your career direction?
- Who chooses your personal brand?

If you can truly say that you have absolute control over these areas, then congratulations. You have hit the motherlode. If, however, there are areas where you are not so sure, maybe you have given or traded away parts of your life to others. Can you really have a beer when you want, or do you have to make sure that your partner doesn't mind? Do the green sandals get thumbs down in front of best customers? Can you choose how much you earn or are you caught in the dead man's shoes trap, where you can only move forward when the next person leaves?

We often exchange choice for comfort, security and guaranteed benefit. If you have traded partial control of your rudder to someone else, then to what extent can you float yourself? To float yourself you need to be able to call the shots when it matters.

We can choose to choose

OK. To recap. The Float You process will work best when you are aware of the choice parameters in your life. Where you trade choice for security, for example. Because you may need to regain some control in order to release and exploit your personal potential.

Fine. So how to start? The first principle is that it is not for other people to give you the power of choice. So don't be thankful when someone says they will allow you to go on a course or run your office in a certain way. This is a capability that you already have. You just may not think you do just yet. You have traded away the power to choose in exchange for some other perceived benefits. If they best serve your well-being, great. If not you can change.

The three diagrams in Fig 7.1 indicate how choice can be eroded over time.

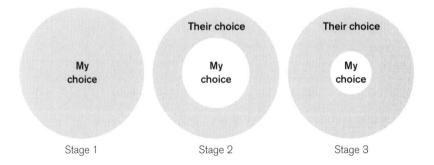

Figure 7.1 *Choice erosion*

Stage 1. As a child you believed you had freedom to make decisions.

As we move into stage 2 the erosion starts. When we start school or work we have to trade some choice in order to not get beaten up in the school playground, be thrown out of the under 7s music class. We have to go with compromise so common operating standards are achieved. Major social training goes on. No more mummy answering our every question. No more only person in the universe. No – one of 20, one of 40. Things change. Stage 3, the natural progression of that social training. Choices go in exchange for the promise of a profession, promotion and pension. We choose survival according to the big plan called normal life. And all the outcomes available to you seem a foregone conclusion somedays. (I get debt or I get this boss; I get life with Steve the Snorer or I get lonely. Oh dear.)

The net result is that we are in the choice trap. We have given away some freedom to make choices. But the good news again is that we can recover them. In fact the Darwinian step forward for you is to recover your powers of choice. Although in the short term there may be some giving up of the traps – not trappings – of success that you so eagerly pursued.

But how to do it? How to get choice back? Like any underused muscle you are going to have to learn to stretch and use it a bit more. First stretch coming up – drawing a choice boundary.

With this you consider what choices you will require to float yourself and what steps need to be taken to get to that level. The first step is to draw two circles – in the inner one write those aspects of your life where you currently choose your choice. Where you feel free to make the decisions. In the outer circle indicate those aspects chosen for you by others.

When complete, you should end up with two pictures like those shown in Fig. 7.2.

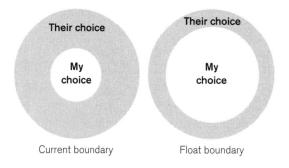

Current boundary   Float boundary

Figure 7.2 *Choice test*

It is important to understand the extent to which you have given away your freedom of choice, what level of choice is appropriate for your personal float process, and what you are prepared to do to redress any imbalance.

The essence of choice within the float you process can be seen as:

1 It is not for other people to give you freedom of choice. Your life started wth a full box of choices. You may have chosen to barter away this choice in exchange for other benefits. Although you may feel that your employer has more choice (or, for that matter your education system, your healthcare provider – whoever you perceive to have more choices than you do in your life), they really don't. The only choices they have over your life are the ones you gave them in the first place.

2 The life you have today is a product of the choices you have taken. The life you want tomorrow will be achieved with the choices you take today. Choose your float choices carefully.

Know where you're going

OK, now you have figured out that you do have some choice. Scary stuff. You are more able than you thought. And with ability comes responsibility (ability plus response equals responsibility) equipped as you are with the capability to choose your choice and own the decision-making process.

Next questions. Do you have a clear idea of what choices need to be taken to aid the float process? What is your criteria for taking them; how do you know when to say yes and when to say no; how do you decide what choices will take you away from a good personal flotation and what will take you towards a great flotation?

But, I hear you ask, *what if I don't know*? What if I don't know what I want? This is the situation known as being alive: somewhere between our last action and our next set of choices. Making decisions or letting someone else make them for us. How about trying this, to try to work out *what you really want to do with your life*.

Your life includes some things you really care about. You love snowboarding. Or working out complex theories about why things happen in the natural world. Or you love being the comedian. Or organising stuff. Or you have some great mechanical skills and love taking things apart to understand how they work. The 'care' elements possess the potential direction for your life's work. What are the things you really enjoy doing, really feel allow you to express your best talents? These 'care' elements are very important to identify. Can you figure out a few of your own?

Next are the aspects of your life over which you have some influence. Some things in life are not in your control – yet. You can, for example, choose to study for another year and get a qualification in a language. You may not be financially able to live in another country while you do it.

It is a kindness to yourself to be realistic about your options, rather than be an extreme high-hoper who lives with a lot of disappointment. Unless you consciously enjoy the drama! Otherwise you risk being buffeted around by the perceived wisdom of others, and as a consequence end up in a place where others think you should be, not where you want to be. The goals you choose really should be right for you, not showbiz to keep others happy. Why? Because going down that road is like being bounced around. In fact we call it …

Bingo ball behaviour

It is this failure to define clear goals that leads to bingo ball behaviour. Imagine Bingo Ball Billie, a lady who works for a large corporation as an administration assistant. She has a reasonably comfortable life, has no real worries, but has the feeling deep down that she can do more with her life. So she decides that the time has come to climb the promotion ladder and seek career fulfilment by trying to float herself to the top of the corporate pile.

Her first step is to talk with Bob, her manager. Bob's advice is don't bother, he tells her that she is under-qualified and unlikely to get more than one rung up the ladder. After all, he tried it three years ago and failed, so why should she fare any better? Although shaken, she is not stirred from her choice and so decides to talk with her friend, Mary. Mary supports Bob's ideas and agrees that there is little chance of making it as the in-crowd corporate team have the promotion all sewn up. Feeling somewhat dejected, Billie decides that maybe it is not such a good idea after all. However, when she gets home, her partner bolsters her up again and suggests that she really can do it, and 'after all, won't the extra money come in handy?'. So the following day she talks with Steve in personnel. Steve says that it might be possible and suggests that what worked for him was to take a series of qualifications. Although they took six years, it really helped him to get where he is.

At the end of all this feedback, Billie is in a quandary and probably is no better off than where she started. Like the ball in a bingo machine she has let herself be pushed up and down and from side to side in the direction she is taking, as seen in Fig. 7.3. At each step of the way,

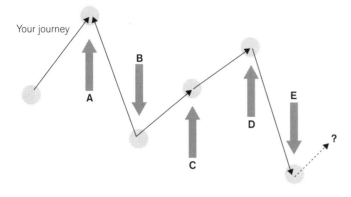

Figure 7.3 *Bingo Ball Billie*

rather than taking the advice as background information, she has taken the other person's view as the right answer and consequently changed her direction. This is like a ship's captain being directed by the crew as he or she tries to bring an oil tanker into a dangerous harbour.

Think about your life. To what extent do you act as a pilot who has absolute control over the direction of the ship, or do you look more like Billie, and simply follow the advice you get from others, indiscriminately? How often do you let other people's views sway your direction? To what extent do you trust the role of experts who claim to understand the future; how often have you decided to avoid an action purely on the basis that someone else tried it and it didn't work? Think about the last big decision you took – it might have been a big purchase or a work decision. How do you decide direction?

Bingo ball behaviour occurs when you don't have a clear outcome in mind. Without a clear destination, it becomes really difficult to know if a piece of advice or guidance really adds to your journey or if it takes you off course.

Bingo ball behaviour occurs when you don't have a clear outcome in mind.

Authors' note: we know this is coming across as a bit John Wayne – sorry. We *do* know that self-change is hard and organic and you need to be gentle with yourself and nurturing. Absolutely. Much more Jane than John Wayne. So if this feels like a good moment for a herbal bath, go right ahead. However, from personal experience, we feel it is also necessary, sometimes, to receive a proverbial kick up the whatsit to get moving. That also works. We want to use anything useful to get you *en route* to Float You. Ok?

Map your map

Having asked all those questions, you should have some clearer view of the float outcome. Now let's get a bit closer to understanding your filters and subjectivity – to try to get even more realism into your float. A fantasy, dream or desire to do something new, different and innovative can be the starting point for any business, social contribution or float. Fantasy is often the pre-requisite in the new economy. Entrepreneurs and innovators are often driven by a dream that powers their personal energy and guides them to the future, irrespective of what other people might say.

The danger is that like any flotation process, only those who actually manage to bubble to the top are hailed as heroes and offered as proof of the ability to make such a journey, forgetting that along the way others have failed abysmally and been left at the bottom. This is often because they have been suckered (or suckered themselves) into using a blueprint or map that is out of date and of little use to anyone. They believed that their dream would be welcomed with open arms by the world and that the flotation would be the making of them. However, they were wrong.

Draw your map

We all have personal maps that express our innermost sense of ourselves and how we make sense of the world. These maps are a set of filtering beliefs that are the foundation of our worldview. (This area is covered in more detail by Stephen Covey in *Seven Habits* (Simon & Schuster, 1999).) If you do want to take yourself through the float process it is worthwhile to first understand these maps, and second, make sure that they are valid, accurate and current. The problem is, maps become a seamless part of us. We assume that what we under-stand to be happening is really happening. When in fact it is just our perception, clouded or sharpened by our personal map of the world.

We see this in both work and personal life. For example, Susan, a hairdresser, moved to a different employer because she believed her current job wasn't making best use of her talents. She moved to another salon, only to find herself in the same dead-end situation but with a different firm. Another example from homelife: someone leaves their partner only to end up in an equally unsatisfying relationship with someone else. Often people will blame the world for these bad experiences, rather than looking inside to understand what maps are being used to guide these failed journeys. So what is going on when this happens?

Any decision to float yourself is based upon your current map of the world. This map is a schema that indicates what is acceptable and unacceptable in your life. It helps you to make decisions about where to move (good district vs. bad district), what to eat (meat or vegetarian), what car to buy (sports vs. saloon). Your map is a mixture of nature and nurture, your inherited family attitudes and your education or life experience. Think about your map and list those things that you believe are acceptable and unacceptable in these various categories:

	Acceptable	Unacceptable
Level of alcohol on a daily basis		
The food I eat		
The transport I use		
The type of work I wish to do		
Where I want to work		
How much I want to earn		

Now consider the list and ask yourself, just where did this judgement come from? How did I build this map of the word? Who influenced these implicit or explicit decisions? Finally, how do I know if they are based on facts or have I built a personal map that is out of touch with the world? How do I know if the decisions I take are based upon fact or fantasy?

We all inhabit a world of perception that is part fact, part fantasy. And all hugely subjective. As this might illustrate.

The question	The answer depends on ...	who you are ...
Are investment banks good for society as a whole?	Yes, for many reasons. For example they add to the invisible earnings of the economy and provide thousands of jobs. *Joe, corporate financier*	No, they allocate capital to the wealthy at preferential rates and deny some developing countries a chance to clear their debt burden. *Paul, aid worker*
Are Russians good at football?	Absolutely. We have the best teams in the world. *Sonia, Moscow*	They're amateurs. They need some proper German coaching. *Beatrice, Munich*
Is it safe to go out in this neighbourhood at night, alone?	No way. I always get a cab after 8.00 pm. *Marty (has been mugged twice in three years)*	No problem as far as I know. *Andy (new to the neighbourhood)*

If you accept that some people live in a dream world and make decisions based upon their fantasy rather than the facts of a situation, how do you know that your decision to go through a float process isn't also based on fantasy? How sure are you that the decisions you have taken are not going to erode your life position rather than enhance it? Can you be sure that any float decision is not going to have a devastating impact on other people in your life who you care for and need to protect? Are things that you take as public facts actually not fantasies that you have constructed to make life seem easier to manage?

Question

Is the person reading this page likely to become very successful (in his/her own terms) in the next few years?	Your mother's view	Your partner's view	What do you think?

Change how you change

Ok. Float outcome identified. You are pretty sure the float is based on fact rather than fantasy. Now, as you go through the next stage of the personal float process there is a need to manage change at a deep and very personal level. Although there are lots of levels of change, a full Float You will cause a holistic life shift. What does that mean? (Is it painful? Can I get cream from the doctor? Sorry.) It simply meant that anyone who embarks on a fully fledged float process is not just changing a part of himself or herself. They are making a significant and lasting shift to the way they think, feel and behave. And in order to achieve a float that is successful and sustainable you will benefit from an understanding of the systemic nature of change and in particular the five levels of personal transformation.

The five levels of change

The five change levels can be seen in the change ladder shown in Fig. 7.4. This is a simple but highly effective tool that will help you to understand the holistic nature of any personal or business transformation. These five levels of change are.

Figure 7.4 Change ladder

We can use the change ladder to look at flotation from a range of perspectives as shown in the list below.

- **Asset.** The tangible elements you need to manage the personal float. This might be the new guitar for the account manager who wishes to form a band to do something different at the weekends, the computer for the parent who wants to go back to work, or the office that the budding entrepreneur needs to build as a base for the new sales team.

- **Blueprint.** This is the method by which you manage how you do things. This might be a new exercise regime for the person who wants to become a fashion model or the business plan for the student who wants to set up a dot.com company.

- **Capability.** These are the skills you use to enact the float. This might be the development of a new range of skills for the office manager who wants to become a management consultant or going to cooking classes for the director who wants to make a life change and open a small restaurant by the coast.

- **Desire.** This is your deep-seated motivation that drives you to undertake the personal float. This might be the desire that you have to leave that safe job after 20 years and finally start your own company or to finally take that degree that you could never take when the children were young.

- **Existence.** This is your sense of purpose, mission or reason for being. Any float process really should align with the sense of who you are and what you wish to do in the world. If you want to give up being a banker and become a chef then you need to understand at a deep level just what this means and how it will impact upon the whole of your life.

Now, let's take the change ladder and consider it in a real situation. Consider someone who has a personal dream to start a charity. There are certain things that really should be considered to ensure that the float process will be successful and sustainable.

Existence The sense of purpose	Define the core purpose of the charity. Agree what it will deliver and those areas it will not tackle.
Desire Motivation to change	Ensure that you have the motivation to carry the plan through, even when friends advise you against the idea. Ensure that you have the motivation to continue, even when other agencies argue against your role. Ensure that you have the motivation to continue even if funds run short and the mortgage will not be paid.
Capability Skills and ability	Ensure you have the skills to run a charity. Learn how to navigate the bureaucratic process to obtain support and funds from government departments, the lottery commission and other charities. Ensure you have the necessary interpersonal skills to build relationships across a wide and diverse range of interest groups.
Blueprint How we operate	Put in place a business plan to manage the start phase of the project. Put in place a process to manage the growth of the charity.
Asset Tangible things	Acquire funds to form the charity. Find offices to house the charity. Order necessary equipment.

Climb the ladder for sustainable change

If you truly want to float yourself, then the first thing to do is climb to the top of the ladder and consider how life will be different. What deep transformation will there be? How will I change? Once you understand what is different ask yourself carefully if you have the courage to make that type or level of change. If not, then maybe it is best not to attempt it right now. Spend more time thinking about what the new you is and what trade-offs you are prepared to make to achieve that outcome. Once you are clear on the change required at the Existence level, then you can start to put in place changes at the Desire, Capability, Blueprint and Asset levels.

It is a failure to manage change across five levels of the change ladder that leads to the New Year's Eve syndrome – where millions of people dream wonderful dreams of their 'new' selves, only to fail with a thundering crash two or three days later when reality hits. Alternatively, for the 2 per cent ready to compound their personal choice into a pattern of change, there can be lasting benefit.

Think about the float you wish to make against the following questions:

Existence	What is the purpose of the float? How resolved are you to this sense of purpose – would you change if there were shifts in the environment or market? What do you hope to achieve?
Desire	What is your motivation? Where has the motivation come from? How strong is your motivation – will you overcome resistance from others?
Capability	Do you have the skills to effect the float? Do you know what skills you will need in the future to make the float last? What skills will others who you are dependent on need to help with the float?
Blueprint	Do you have the plan in place to help you manage the float? Do you have alternatives in place to manage the float if problems occur?
Asset	Do you have all the tangible assets needed to manage the float? Will you be able to continue if you are not able to acquire the assets?

The key to a successful float is the ability to change how you change – which means what exactly? Well, it means losing the change clichés we tell ourselves, without foundation, every now and again. They do more harm than good.

The change ladder is a logical progression so you can assess how likely the whole process is to work – bit by manageable bit. The first change is to climb up the ladder to look at personal transformation from the E rung – considering the higher definition – rather than figuring things will work out in your new business just because you have been offered some plush office space by one of your friends. An asset is not enough. By working on the overall purpose of the float process, you start to understand how to ensure you stay motivated, develop the right capability, put in place plans for change and gather the necessary tools and assets to effect the float.

Step inside out

No person or company can float without the support and guidance of other people. The company that floats has to draw upon a wide range of industry and market experts to help with the market launch. In the same way you will also have to draw upon your friends, colleagues and partners to make any significant transition. So, your goals and float hopes need to be presented in a way that makes sense to other stakeholders and potential partners. To achieve this you might want to figure out how to be able to re-frame and re-format your float proposal and present it in a way that makes sense to others. Therefore you need to step inside out, to virtually step from your world into theirs and see life as they see it.

No person or company can float without the support and guidance of other people.

Multiverse management

We often present our thoughts to others based upon the idea that there is a single right way to do things or, in essence, a single universe. However, we all filter through the subjective lens of our own experience. Therefore at individual level, it is important to realise that our worldview is not the only valid one. Michael Moorcock, a science fiction writer, talks about the idea of a 'multiverse'. The 'multiverse' is a multitude of alternative universes sometimes intersecting with our own and to which, of course, our own belongs – an infinite number of slightly different versions of reality in which one is likely to come across a slightly different version of oneself.

This notion of a multiverse is crucial in the step inside out decision. It is hard to see someone else's problem standing on your side of the fence. However, before you can step inside someone else's world to understand it, you might want to figure out how to believe in your heart and head that their world exists and is related to, but different from, yours.

To accept someone else's view of the world, you should maybe walk in their shoes and see the world as they see it. Accept that they see things differently from you, feel things differently from how you feel them, and act in a different way because that makes sense to them. To do this you will have to re-frame your world orientation – to take a multi-dimensional view of the world. For example, leaders of the US civil rights movement, including Martin Luther King and Rosa Parks, employed hugely empathetic language to reach out to the common humanity of thousands of Americans. In one speech Rev. Luther King suggested the needs of the black community as being similar to a person, waiting in the bank for a cheque to be cashed. He said that the black community 'refuses to believe that the bank of justice is bankrupt'. This and other powerful images awoke a sense of 'it could be me' inside a wide cross-section of the American population. And in time things started to change. So the ability to use powerful 'multiverse' language helped create coalitions which were at the heart of the civil rights movement.

In terms of your float process, this ability to see things from another viewpoint is based on the idea that we can re-frame how we experience the world. And yes, we can repeat that. Each one of us learns to view reality through the lens of experience. And no two world views are the same. In fact, twin brothers can have hugely different worldviews. There is a wealth of experience (especially from the field of Neuro-Linguistic-Programming, or NLP) which states that we can change our world-view, steer the thoughts. It is possible to change the frame in which a person perceives events in order to change the meaning.

Think about your float and consider the following questions.

◆ Who else is involved in your float?

◆ How close are you to them?

◆ Do you understand what is important to them?

◆ How would they describe why you are floating – is it close to your description?

- How important is your float to them?
- What is more important than your float to them and why?

Perhaps think about mapping this – in management the word stakeholder has taken hold. Why don't you list the top three people likely to be impacted by your float, and just try to see things through their eyes. From that, try to assess pros and cons of the float.

Stakeholder matrix

People impacted by my float	Likely benefits for that person	Likely disadvantages	Overall – is my float good or bad for this person?
My best mate			
My son/daughter			
My business partner			

This isn't luxury touchy feely stuff. Unless you are able to climb inside their universe, understand how they view your situation, then you will not be able to truly ensure that the people you care about, your float stakeholders, are on board and able and willing to help in any change that you wish to make.

Share success

In a world of fudge and mumble, you can trust the float authors to come straight at ya! Ready? Ok.

Personal flotation that is selfish and short-lived is unlikely to be truly effective. The only effective float is one founded in the notion of shared outcomes and sustainable success. Got that? Or, put another way, it is possible to exploit and manipulate your way to some success, but there are going to be structural flaws which will cause the float to be short-lived. *Built to Last* (Collins and Porras, Random House, 1998) showed this at organizational level.

Firms with lasting values and principles stay strong for longer – measured on stock market performance. Your float is no different. The key to this choice is your absolute focus on the goal of mutual benefit. Success is not about individual achievement. Successful flotation is a shared experience connected with lots of people.

To achieve this you should maybe know:

◆ what you wish to achieve as part of your flotation
◆ who the people are that have a role to play in your flotation network
◆ what their success factors are
◆ how to bridge the difference between your need and their needs to deliver a shared outcome.

However, the capability to generate a successful flotation is often driven more by the hidden issues that impact a relationship. Factors like:

- the extent to which you share the same values and beliefs as the other person
- the extent to which you demonstrate care and consideration for each other
- the extent to which you understand and demonstrate the value the other person brings to the relationship.

These three variables offer a significant contribution to the success of any relationship, and failure to deal with or talk about one of the factors can limit the opportunity to realise a successful flotation.

As you start to think about the practical aspects of working with others to achieve your flotation, ask yourself, what values do I really share with these people I work with; to what extent do we demonstrate how valued they are, and to what extent do we appreciate the value we offer each other in the relationship? The three factors come together as the V-ness factors.

your float strategy

float you

momentum

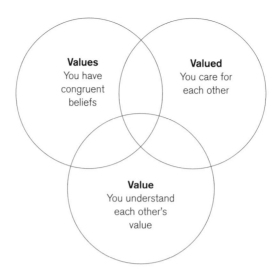

Figure 7.5 *The V-ness factors*

Values

At the heart of any organization, family or social group are the deep values of the individuals who make up the culture. For example, one person values freedom highly. Her circle of friends reflects this – she hangs out with people who prioritize career flexibility, love of travel, with less emphasis on material possessions. It is the rich range of personal and shared beliefs that bind people together, push them apart, and generally make the world go round. Hence, we should maybe be sure that the values of the people, teams and organization are related in such a way as to facilitate the ability to share success wherever we are. Shared success can only be truly realized when there is an alignment between the values you hold and those of your networks. Consider if your values are shared or unique, aligned or out of synch with those of your float stakeholders.

My values – what is most important to me	Values held to be most important to a float stakeholder – my sister	Values held to be most important to a float stakeholder – my partner
Family	**Family**	**Family**
Freedom	Security	Freedom
Creativity	Respect	Challenge
Justice	Health/well-being	Professional development

How do your priority values line up with those of your float
stakeholders? In the example shown above, using a top four, my
values align with those of my sister to about 25 per cent. With my
partner about 50 per cent. Value alignment ratios could be a tool of
the network generation – or is it just over-egging the pudding? You
get the idea – just try to understand how much you have in common.
It matters.

Valued

What is it that makes you give the best of yourself? What is it that
makes you go that extra mile to make the relationship and the task
work that bit better; what is it that makes you want to work with
someone a second or third time even if the previous projects didn't
quite deliver all that was expected? It is often because you feel that
the other person, team or organization values you personally and the
work you put into a task. For example, simply saying thank you.
Thanks and expressions of gratitude oil the wheels. The primary idea
with this part of the V-ness model is twofold. First, most of us need
to feel valued. Second, it is within all our power to give strokes of
recognition to people who we want to feel valued. It costs nothing,
but real rewards seal relationships and can help deliver real
sustainable shared success.

Value

As you go through the float process you will be trading your
personal capital with the world as a form of soft currency. You will
gain access to people and network opportunities based on your
ability to offer something of value to others. Therefore ask yourself
the question, what is it that I trade with the world to create success
and what value will I need from others to make the float successful?

Once you understand this, are you able to determine the market value of the personal capital and agree a rate with other people? This point is critical because a shared success with imbalanced reward will limit its chance of renewal. If one person believes that they are not receiving fair and equitable reward for their effort, then distraction and disquiet will arise and the sustainability of the shared success will be eroded over time.

Or put another way, if you feel ripped off, you don't want to play anymore. No matter how nicely you get asked.

The challenge for us all is to be sensitive to the balance of the V-ness factors. We need to be tuned into our preferences, the preferences of others and the environment in general. If there is an imbalance or conflict across our values, how we feel valued, and how we reward value, then this should maybe be understood so that the chance to share a successful flotation can be eroded.

The challenge for you is to ensure that other people feel valued, feel rewarded for their contribution in helping your float, and feel able to share their values with you. By understanding and managing these three factors you can share success with hardly any effort on your part but create a huge success for others.

level 2
know your value

How do you manage your time? Generally, the answer to the question will range from a filofax or PDA (otherwise known as Personal Digital Assistant); right through to 'I keep a scrap of paper on the fridge.' How do you manage your finances? Again, the answer will vary, from the use of a personal financial account package on the PC, to 'I spend what I earn.' How do you manage your value? ... In most cases, people respond with a cough, they look blank, and maybe mention the Open University course they are taking, or their latest personal development workshop.

Few people are able to explain clearly and lucidly how they manage and maintain their personal market value. By market value we mean the following:

- how they acquire new knowledge
- grow their intellectual capital
- leverage this value to support their personal float.

Many people would be upset if they were asked to relinquish control of their time or financial management system, but seem happy to leave the management of their personal capital to other people. As we move into the knowledge era, this is not the best situation to be in.

The know your value stage in the float process is designed to help you understand and define your market worth or value. This is specifically about your value and not the value of the float idea you are taking to market. To understand the perceived market value of your ideas, your skill, and your ability to create emotional relationships, and this impacts upon the potential success of the float.

This is a new way of thinking and the question is, how to start?

To know your value you should maybe start by identifying the qualities or characteristics that make you distinctive from your competitors – or your colleagues, or float peers. What do you do that is different from others, what do others love about you, what makes you stand out? What would your family or customers say is your greatest and clearest contribution? What is your most noteworthy personal trait or habit?

Ask yourself: What do I do that is of value and valued by others? Ignore the corporate ladder of progression you may have climbed in your career up to now. What have you done outside of that you can unashamedly shout about? To know your value, you'll need to become passionate about managing, mapping and measuring the unique things you do that add value, things you're proud of, and most importantly, that you can brazenly take credit for.

Signpost

- **Vote value not price.** Price is different from value. The price you receive should always be driven by the value of your personal capital. Whereas in many cases people believe that the price they receive is an indication of their value in the market.

- **Powered by personal capital.** Personal capital is just that. It is something that you own and have every right to market and set a price for. Before you can do this you will need to understand just what your stock of capital is.

- **Dig deeper.** Once you understand how your capital is held you can understand how you apply it in the market and how best to optimize its value.

- **Audit your assets.** Some of your assets might help to create value in the market whereas others might reduce your value. When you audit and map the status and market view of your assets you improve your chance of trading your value in a marketplace where it is wanted and valued.

◆ **Benchmark your value.** Although you might place a price on the value of your personal capital, this may carry little weight in the market. Ultimately the marketplace drives value/price ratio. So it pays to carry out benchmark activities to ensure that your valuation compares favourably.

◆ **Position your value.** The type of market in which you operate drives the ultimate value of your capital. Therefore valuation depends upon whether you are in a niche or commodity market. This is a key determinant of the price you receive for your personal capital.

Vote value not price

If you take one idea from this section, it should be that price is not the same as value. The price you pay for a bottle of water is not its value. Ask someone who lives in a hot and dusty village in Tunisia. The price you pay for an umbrella is not its value. Ask someone caught in a rainstorm in the middle of winter. Most importantly the price that someone places on you for the work you do (your company, boss, partner) is not your value, it is simply a transaction price agreed at that moment in time for that work.

The Float You process helps you ask whether the price you are currently being sold for in the market is the same as your value. The essence of Float You is to ensure that the price you receive is a fair and equitable recognition of your value.

If you take one idea from this section, it should be that price is not the same as value.

But what is value? What is the fair value of a stock, painting or second-hand car? The answer to this question depends on investor expectations for earnings or pleasure gained from acquiring the asset. The price paid for two comparable similar items can vary widely according to the worth placed on each item by the investor. Paintings of approximately the same size, subject matter and competence done in the same medium, will have vastly differing price-tags. The reality is that the name of the painter ranks first among those factors which count in the establishment of value. Ask yourself, what is the value of your name, brand or reputation in relation to your float? Past performance predicts future performance. Are you a marketable commodity that people will clamber to invest in and support, are you a fledgling newbie that people don't really know and will be loath to take a risk in supporting; or are you seen as a has-been, someone that has floated yourself so many times that this one will never really provide a return on the investment?

Other people will generally take you at your own estimation of your worth. Your life circumstances mirror your thinking. If you limit yourself to roles that do not provide any excitement or sense of meaning, then guess what, that is the work that others will place you in. If you go for an interview and fill the room with self-limiting value beliefs then the interview panel will trust your judgement and place you in the job position that fits the bill. If you are able to present a self-valuation to the world that shows your talent, then although you can't guarantee you will receive the asking price, at least others might accept and negotiate based on the valuation you place upon yourself.

Powered by personal capital

The ability to float yourself is driven and supported by the extent to which you are able to harness and market your personal capital. Let's consider the idea of personal capital to start with.

The notion of capital is not generally linked with the word personal. Capital is something that companies or governments need to fund growth or pay debts, isn't it? Yes, it is. However, we are witnessing a shift towards an individualized economic order. What you do and who you know matters as much as your business or school or family ties. To use one example, for highly paid media performers, personal knowledge, personal attributes and personal choice reign supreme. A Hollywood labour dispute recently bore this out. Actors and writers and directors realized that cheaper labour simply could not be substituted because the personal capital of each striker was too valuable, too unique. We believe this has implications for everyone. Each one of us needs to control our personal capital in the same way that a financial director will guard the financial assets of the business. And this is a big shift.

The ability to float yourself is driven and supported by the extent to which you are able to harness and market your personal capital.

The process of becoming more personal value savvy has two distinct aspects. The first investigates the current structure of your life, to unearth the value you may have buried. The value savvy person is focused on long-term benefit. Activities are viewed as investments in new production capability that will generate future value. The value savvy person will often be able to take a more objective view of their life, stepping outside their world view to take dispassionate choices about investment decisions. They will consider when on a train journey whether reading a book on personal taxation will release more or less benefit than writing a paper for the next office meeting. They will weigh up spending two hours building sales prospects against developing the next round of products. These are all investment decisions that someone who knows and cares for their value will consciously rather than sub-consciously take.

By focusing on value creation as a daily activity, people become better equipped to tune themselves into the market. This means fewer nasty surprises – like drastically changing their life when turbulence hits the market and they have to find a new job.

The immediate result from this action can range from moderate improvement to magnificent achievement. It might be a significant increase in wages, more clients for your business or growth in demand from people who want to work with you. However, this is all the up side. There can be difficult aspects as well. By taking such a focused view on value-added activities in your life, you will be less willing to spend time on areas or people in your life that don't add to your success and happiness. This is why it is so important to complete the know yourself level before embarking on this level. Reading level one will help you decide direction and focus as to what and who is important in your life.

Paula's story

Let's consider potential Paula's personal capital. She has completed an adult literacy programme and started a pre-university entry course. The world is her oyster but she still feels under ten feet of water. Although feels like she is drowning, in fact she doesn't realize just how much of an asset she is to herself. For a start she has worked in a range of industries and companies and has a good, explicit understanding of the different techniques used to run a business. She therefore picks up new job processes and procedures really quickly. At a tacit (meaning deeper, uncoded) level she has a deep understanding of how to build good working relationships. Although she doesn't know how she does it. Where does this come from? It might be because of time spent as a first-aid assistant in an overseas youth camp, dealing with a whole range of problems with a diverse bunch of children.

These are just two examples of the personal capital Paula has at her disposal, which is not being marketed or valued explicitly in the market. It isn't being valued because Paula doesn't know these things about herself, or the potential market application of her value.

In the same way, we suggest that fewer than 2 per cent of the population – if asked – could say how they measure their personal capital value. How much it is worth and how they market it to the world. Instead, so many of us just take the easy way out and let others tell us what we are worth. When we do that I suggest that 'the others' will often not understand the value of our capital and consequently devalue our price in the market.

In the next part of this chapter we will help you to identify the different elements which make up your personal capital. Your personal capital is a combination of your explicit and tacit stock of capital. Think of these two forms of stock as being like goods stacked in a warehouse, ready to be shipped to happy customers. Tacit is the knowledge it took to get the goods made and stored, the deeply embedded ways of working that come with habit and a long time doing it. Think of explicit stock as being like the warehouse plan and how to use the forklift to put goods on a pallet.

Added to that are the ways that you express those explicit and tacit areas of stock. These can be intellectual, behavioural and emotional currencies that enable you to take yourself to market and trade with the world. Think of these as the team communication that ensures smooth working in the warehouse. These concepts will become clearer as we go through each in more detail.

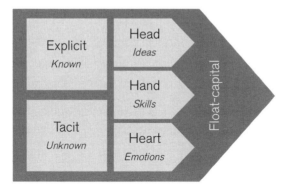

Figure 8.1 *Personal Capital Layer Model*

Explicit stock

This is the value that you are able to know and describe. Explicit knowledge can be expressed in words and numbers, is easily communicated and shared in the form of hard data, scientific formulae, codified procedures or universal principles. This is hard, tangible knowledge that can be codified, replicated and readily transferred across an organization. It is the content of books, reports, newspapers. It is the safety instructions before the plane takes off. For your float it might be how you describe what the float is, the economic evaluation of how you will do it, your plan, and your personal stakeholders.

Tacit stock

This is the innate or intuitive value that you use to support the float but can't quite describe what or how you do it. It is in the fingertips or muscle capability – where you perform a task but find it difficult to explain how. It can be the knowledge you don't know you have, for example, how to open a door may not seem like 'knowledge' until you meet somebody who has never seen a door.

One simple way to describe tacit knowledge is in the phrase 'we can know more than we can tell'. Another way to describe it is 'the answer to questions that haven't been asked yet'. Whatever definition is used, it is that which we apply and use, but have yet to codify in a way such that we can describe how we perform that action. Look at any individual; ask them to describe what they do and how they do it. The guarantee is that you will only gain a partial appreciation of their unique skills and knowledge. The tacit element is probably unable to be described. Ask any artist to explain their unique use of colour, or ask the tennis player how their magical drop shot works!

All of these elements are buried deep within the individual. It can be difficult to transform this deep personal capital into a codified form. It is for this very reason that tacit knowledge is highly prized within the float process. By building a market advantage around your tacit knowledge base, it more or less ensures that competitors will find it difficult to replicate your market offering. As such, tacit knowledge is more likely to be a source of competitive advantage than the explicitly articulated knowledge.

Now we have explored the tacit and explicit stock, let's look at the next way of unravelling your personal capital and the way that you take both explicit and tacit stock and communicate them in the marketplace. These are the currency areas.

Head currency

Head currency is our cognitive ability. This is often viewed as our intelligence or general mental ability. It refers to our capacity to process information and to use such information to manage behaviour.

This act of knowledge and processing can be split into many areas. These include:

◆ problem diagnostics and interpretation, which is the ability to discriminate between factors and take the appropriate decision based upon the evidence

◆ numerical or verbal ability, which might be seen in the capability to understand and arrange ideas according to a certain set of patterns and rules

◆ visual or spatial interpretation, or the ability to perceive and visualize objects in space. This capability is not limited to a few of the more common intellectual areas that are normally included in the bracket of intelligence.

Whereas most intelligence tests have focused on the ability to reason and calculate, there are many other forms of intelligence that we need to consider when thinking about the head element. One Harvard professor suggests that we have many types of intelligence, including linguistic, logical, musical, kinaesthetic, visual, spatial, interpersonal and intrapersonal. This highlights the need to really understand how we mentally process things and more importantly how we use these mental processes to deliver the float idea.

Hand currency

We all use skills and behaviours to express ourselves, to essentially trade with the world. These are all the activities, responses, reactions, movements and processes, operations that we use to perform our jobs. For the mechanic it is the ability to use a set of tools, the juggler, dexterity with a set of balls, for the computer technician the ability to take apart and reassemble a personal computer.

If we look at behaviour as a currency to be exchanged and bartered in the world, we might look at the transaction process. We can start to ask questions such as, how do I acquire my skills and behaviours; how do I know what skills are worth acquiring? How do I create a market for my skills? What value should I place on my ability to perform a function for someone else? Through these questions we can see the process of behavioural acquisition and delivery as a buy/sell process. We buy new skills by attending a course; this adds to our personal value and experience; so we sell these improved skills to the market for a higher rate. Germane to this is being able to identify your real hand assets. Our CV or résumé lists various competencies and skills we can offer to the market. We might list 'project management' as a skill on the CV and leave it as that. But as part of the float process (which in case you had forgotten, is making sure you optimize your personal capital value) it is important to consider at a deeper level. What skills are required to manage a project? Negotiation, listening, presenting, influencing etc. Of these capabilities how effective are you at each and what market value might be placed on them as distinct elements of the successful project manager? To understand the value of your personal capital, it is important to understand in some detail how you create market value and dig deeper than generic job titles. People will buy the top negotiator out of a range of similiarly qualified project managers. You might be that top negotiator, but you didn't realize it – it was buried somewhere in your experience but you hadn't worked it out. And therefore couldn't express your ability to the interview panel. Therefore someone less able than you was selected. And therefore, it really does matter.

Heart currency

This is the personal capital that you draw on to both motivate yourself and build effective relationships with others. It might be seen in two areas, inter- and intra-emotional capability:

Intra-emotional capability – to manage oneself

◆ Knowing your internal states, preferences, resources and intuitions.

◆ Self-confidence: having a sense of your own worth and capability.

◆ Self-control, keeping control of your internal emotions, impulses and intuition.

- Trustworthiness: maintaining standards of honesty and integrity.

- Flexibility in the way you deal with change.

- Goal focused with the necessary drive to reach goals and desired outcomes.

- Initiative: readiness to act on opportunities.

- Persistence in pursuing goals despite obstacles and setbacks.

Inter-emotional capability – to manage the relationship with others

- Awareness of others' feelings, needs and concerns.

- Empathy and ability to sense others' feelings and perspectives and be aware of their needs.

- Developing others: sensing others' development needs and bolstering their abilities.

- Cultivating opportunities through different kinds of people.

- Group sensitivity – tuning into a group's emotional currents and power relationships.

- Influencing others to change direction.

- Listening openly and sending convincing messages.

- Negotiating skills and leadership to inspire and guide individuals and groups.

- Collaboration with others toward shared goals.

If you don't know and 'value' your own capital – how on earth can you expect others to?

Dig deeper

Just imagine someone who is 39 years old, has worked in engineering all his life and has just been told that he is about to be made redundant. He starts to think, 'what on earth can I do? All I know is how to be an engineering manager and in this area that is the last thing people need.' In his mind, the life he had carefully constructed has just been blown apart.

For as long as he thinks in this way, aligning his worth with the job that he undertook, then his value will be limited. However, if he digs deeper he can understand some of the undiscovered capital he has access to.

Considering the capital factors covered already, he has a stock of explicit and tacit capability and also a range of currencies (how he thinks, behaves and feels) that he exchanges with the world. If we take these factors and integrate them, we can start to define just what it is that he brings to the world and maybe start to consider how to place a more realistic value on it.

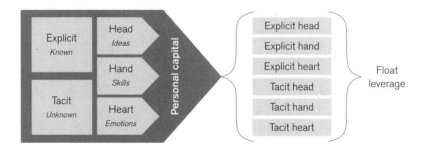

Figure 8.2 *Layer model*

The two stock aspects of explicit and tacit can be seen to occur at all three currency levels (head, hand and heart) to produce the six-layer personal capital framework shown in Fig. 8.2. This is the underlying structure that can be used to understand how to fully leverage your personal value to float in the market. It deconstructs your personal capital in a way that we hope will help you define how to apply some of the intangible elements of your personal capital. The six levels might be described as below:

Personal capital	Description
Explicit head	The ideas about the float you can describe.
Explicit hand	The skills and competencies you know about.
Explicit heart	The known strategies and tactics you use to motivate yourself and create relationships.
Tacit head	The underlying mental models or assumptions you use to manage the float.
Tacit hand	The intuitive skills and capabilities used to deliver the float.
Tacit heart	Your innate capability to set personal goals and work with others.

These six factors make up your personal capital and ultimately your capability to float yourself and your idea in the market.

The goal is to take each of the six levels in the personal capital framework and understand how to use them to leverage your float forward. How do you leverage the explicit and tacit ideas that you have? To what extent are your skills going to help at an explicit and tacit level, and in what way will your explicit and tacit emotion capital aid the process?

Now take the model shown above and see if you can list your assets for each of the six levels in the personal capital model. Take each box and try to describe the one core value that you have in that domain. If you can't find the right world, try asking a friend or colleague just what they value about you in the six areas.

Explicit head

This is the information that you are able to express using language or some other type of communication. You might discover this knowledge by reading books, watching TV, talking with friends and colleagues or simply reflecting on life and coming up with a new invention that in turn leads to your float idea.

> **Personal capital – explicit head**
> I have the following knowledge that will help with my float:

Explicit hand

These are the known skills that you have to enable the float. This might be seen in the skills that a keynote presenter uses to engage and electrify the audience, or how the footballer scores a goal from the halfway line.

> **Personal capital – explicit hand**
> I have the following skills and knowledge that will help with my float:

Explicit heart

This is less visible than the previous two, although in many ways it can offer greater value. The capability to deliver value in this area means that you have the ability to manage your own emotions and those of other people effectively. You are able to outline your personal goals, ambitions, desires and values. You can work with others to understand theirs and how the two can be aligned.

Personal capital – explicit heart
I have the following emotional capability that will help with my float:

Tacit head

Very often we will take actions or decisions without really understanding why or how we took them. This is because we have deep-seated mental models or frames of reference that guide how we operate in the world. You might find it difficult to quickly explain or codify exactly what these beliefs are, but given time you might be able to.

In the same way, look around any organization and there will be artefacts, processes and systems that indicate the tacit structure that underlies the rules and regulations of the business. In one company the MD might wish to have sight of all expense claims submitted by the sales teams, in another they might be signed off by the individual's line manager. This gives a strong indication of the tacit ideas that are being used by the MD. Whereas one believes in delegated responsibility, the other might take a more centralized view. Now tacit head models will underpin your whole float process and they will impact upon the success of your change. As such it is important to understand what these models are prior to the float and what they need to evolve into to best support the transformation.

Personal capital – tacit head
I have the following deep assumptions that will help with my float:

Tacit hand

This is the way we naturally behave when presenting ourselves to the market. Think of the last time you watched a TV presenter.

Although many of their skills might have been professionally honed by attending a training course, there will still have been elements that were intuitively their own. The way they talked, or the facial expressions to camera are both indications of the tacit behaviour. These are things that we do quite intuitively. It is possible to change tacit behaviour, but it will generally take time and might mean some hard work to ensure its sustainability.

Personal capital – tacit hand
I have the following habits that will help with my float:

Tacit heart

Consider someone who has just attended a relationship management course and returned to work in the firm belief that they can now work with anyone. However this embodiment of diplomacy and optimism hits a problem trying to put the theory into action. Why? Because although they use all the techniques, they still fail to improve their relationships. This is because techniques might help deal with short-term issues, such as how to coach someone and give some critical feedback in a constructive way but techniques cannot overcome a basic inability to form effective relationships. Tacit heart capability is a deep ability to foster good relationships and be self-motivating. This component is interesting because it is the one area that is rarely discussed in a commercial setting, but possibly has the most impact on our effectiveness.

Personal capital – tacit heart
I have the following deep emotional capability that will help with my float:

Audit your assets

Ok, so what does this mean?

An audit might be defined as a process to conduct an independent review and examination of a system in order to test its adequacy and effectiveness. To also ensure compliance with established policy and operational procedures, and to recommend any necessary changes. An audit also serves as an examination of the system after an event to adjust the stock levels and identify the gap between what exists and what should exist.

Oh, so what does this *really* mean?

For example, when colleges award a degree they are auditing the candidate's level of knowledge to assure and evaluate the level of knowledge acquired during the programme. It might be seen as a programme that provides the capability of evaluating a student's course and exam work, and determining whether degree specifications have been satisfied.

Ok, so what does this really mean for *you*?

There is little point in Lisa deciding to give up her current career and start her own web design firm if she is severely lacking in one of the areas on the personal capital framework. For example if she is unable to control her perceived irritability with dissent (tacit hand) or grasp the basic of HTML coding (explicit head) then such a move might be foolish and therefore not encouraged by those who have been asked to support her transformation. There is also little point in Martin spending five years at night school to attain an MBA if he believes that being a director will require little change in the way he works with his current colleagues and friends (tacit head).

However, this is not to suggest that a weakness in these areas means that the float should not proceed. It simply means that Martin and Lisa have a clearer understanding of their improvement areas. They can choose to focus some effort on these, to ensure their float is successful. Therefore, the essence of knowing your value is to undertake a personal audit to determine the strength of your current assets against the capability required to undertake the float.

Within your float process, and particularly at the know your value stage, it is important that you set up a process to independently assure yourself that you have all the necessary personal capital to make the float. This is like the pre-flight checklist that pilots will undertake before setting off around the world. They know that they have all the necessary fuel, equipment and instrumentation to start the journey, but they will still run through a checklist to audit or assure them that they are ready and prepared for the journey.

In the same way it is important that you create a discrete process that defines what you will need to float and ritually test yourself against this criteria.

Change activist personal capital audit

In an earlier book by one of us (*Change Activist*, momentum, 2001) there's a summary of key skills you'll need to make the float happen. How do we know this? Well, not for certain, but these skills are common to a number of social and business activists. These are all successful people who changed history. So they seem like useful tutors for another now float safety check.

Evaluate yourself against to each of the seven points below, in relation to your chosen objective. Next to each write down a strength and any development needed. Write this against all seven.

Describe a situation where you demonstrated these skills. What evidence exists? Get data by talking with friends and colleagues on their view of your readiness for change. Importantly, just listen. Don't justify or defend. Feedback is as useful as cash if you want to float.

The activist audit

1 Clarity of objective

Personal review

- Ability to think of the wider context

- The ability to make decisions quickly
  and act quickly

- Clear thinking, intellectual confidence
  and analytical skills

2 Motivation and motivational leadership

Personal review

- Dedication and perseverance
  sometimes to an extreme

- Leadership skills – influencing,
  negotiating, listening, ability to
  modify behaviour based on feedback

3 Trust and care – emotional intelligence

Personal review

- A relationship builder, using trust
  and emotional intelligence

- Confidence to take risks and at
  times be unpopular

4 Inclusive ways of working

Personal review

- Recognition of diversity, respect for
  all contributors

- The ability to create/belong to an
  effective team

your float strategy

float you

momentum

5 Communication

Personal review

◆ Being a motivational communicator
  – speechmaker, copywriter

◆ Listening – to the world, to the
  organization, to yourself

6 Sense of self-esteem and self-worth in the world

Personal review

◆ Clarity on career/life objectives

◆ Personal centredness and positive
  self-esteem

7 Motivation and motivational leadership

Personal review

◆ Speaks for itself

How was that? Now if we told you that you were benchmarking your capability against Ghandhi, Nelson Mandela, Mohammed Yunus, Anita Roddick and A. John Bird, how would that make you feel? Pretty good, we hope. You are comparing yourself to people who have changed the world and been examples of moral leadership.

Now try to build your audit checklist. What is your pre-flight check and how will you know that you are ready to jump when the time comes?

Benchmark your value

Ok, you understand the makeup of your personal capital. Great. Now let's help you understand the value that you and the market place on it. This is not a science. You unfortunately can't multiply a few numbers together, add a coefficient and get an accurate market valuation. This is an art and one difficult to master, primarily because (as we outlined earlier) it is the market view, not yours, that counts.

What was the market value a few hours before Gerald Ratner made his famous comment on the value of the jewellery in his stores compared to his market value once the papers broke the story? (Ratner, then the chairman, described his company's products as 'crap' and the market valued shares accordingly. He soon left.)

Market value is expressed in ways other than cash. In politics and in many socially active professions the leaders have to retain high stock value inside the organization. How did the low personal stock value of Peter Mandelson contribute to his political downfall? If his personal stock had been higher, is it possible that his errors would have been judged differently by the leadership of the UK Government? With few senior allies and several enemies, he was forced to resign from Cabinet for a second time. Personal stock value, expressed as support and solidarity, can sometimes be more valuable than any amount of cash.

On a more domestic level, how do you find out the value of your house? You look around and find comparable houses, some a bit better and some a bit worse. You note the valuations and this benchmark gives you a value to fix your house against. How does a football manager determine the value of a footballer who is on the market? Again they will look at comparable skills and potential performance from other players and from this determine a market worth.

So there are lots of ways of benchmarking value. At a personal level, the secret is to deconstruct your personal capital into discrete units to understand the value and worth of each asset level. What are your published ideas worth? How much do people value your practised skills as a bartender or carpenter or academic? To what extent is your market value dependent upon your ability to form good, trusting relationships? When you understand the market worth of each of these assets, it becomes possible to assemble the separate values into a potential market value.

Know how to know your value

1 Check salaries and reward polices to know what value is given in the area where you wish to float.

2 Research and note opportunities for people with your personal capital assets – in the same company, in different companies, in different industries, in different parts of the industry, in different countries, etc.

3 Become an expert at translating your personal assets and skills into promotable market benefits. Practise your one-minute 'float story' until it convinces your friends and relatives.

4 Immerse yourself in the float area – know its environment, its needs, its trends. Be ready to leverage your personal capital when you see an opportunity.

5 Join trade associations, online discussion panels, committees and read trade publications and the business press to develop a good understanding of how value is measured and marketed. There's no better way to assess your value than to get feedback from other people in the business.

6 Understand how market pay and reward is set in the arena where your float will take place. Understand how human resources or purchasing departments establish their policies and how flexible they are.

This is by no means an exhaustive list, but it is an excellent start for your research.

Position your value

Once you have an idea of the worth of your personal capital, the next stage is to think about how you position yourself in the market. Marketing position is driven by two primary factors, the extent to which you are able to differentiate your float and the price you ask. Although there are many other factors that contribute to the market mix, these two make for a fast, realistic picture. We can use these two factors to develop the matrix shown in Fig. 8.3.

This is a market position model that challenges you to think about where you sit at the moment and where you want to sit in future, so as to fully exploit your personal capital.

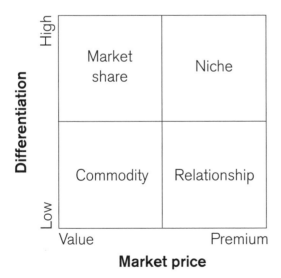

Figure 8.3 *Market position matrix*

You can opt to be in any one of the four boxes. It depends on how much you, and the market, value your personal capital. This applies to the person wanting to get promoted inside the internal market of a large organization; it applies to the entrepreneur with a new service offering. Both need to be correctly positioned within their respective marketplaces.

First of all, what is your current marketplace?

Comparing our float candidates

Lisa's marketplace – potential buyers of web design and maintenance, both corporate and private

Martin's marketplace – the investment bank he works in, plus bank customers and suppliers

Paula's marketplace – in a year's time, she will be applying for a place at university. So that will be a kind of marketplace (although not all criteria apply). Currently, employers able to provide some part-time earnings while she studies.

And your current marketplace? What is your source of earnings, your wider potential source of earnings? What is the environment you'll have to navigate in order to achieve your float goal?

Ok, now you are located in your own marketplace, let's look at your positioning options.

The four options are:

Commodity
Here you operate in a market that will generally have low entry barriers, but with the trade-off that it will not generate significant margins. The upside is that with low start-up costs, you have the flexibility to enter and withdraw from the market without taking a major risk. The downside is that it can be quite a battle, as there are lots of others in there with you! Examples of roles in this market include jobs to be found in most employment centres or job agencies.

Market share
In this segment, you enter the market as a specialist but with a low price position. The upside is that it offers the chance to get your personal brand known quickly in the market and to recoup some early revenue on your investment costs. The downside is that you

incur a degree of risk. If your specialist area requires a lot of start-up investment and you cannot generate the appropriate returns, you risk falling at the first hurdle.

Relationship

One way to move into this is by spending time building trust and, softly softly, understanding the key market needs. It can pay to develop relationships with the market players and only then move to a position where you sell your personal products. This is a classic marketing model. The upside of this approach can be locked into a long-term revenue stream. The downside can be an over-dependence that could prove disastrous if the relationship is lost for some reason.

Niche

Finally, it is possible to generate a premium return by offering a product that is unique in the marketplace. Your ability to differentiate at a personal level or company level can build long-term revenue streams. The downside is that markets can be fickle and change over night. Yesterday's new thing is today's discount line. So, if you follow this strategy, ensure you build in contingency plans.

This four-market position model doesn't seek to say which is the right market entry point, rather it is to challenge you to think about your personal capital at a level of detail. Can you position your offering within the four boxes? Do you feel comfortable or is it better to change your market positioning? This is about learning that you can negotiate with the marketplace. Your value is your value and you don't want to give it away.

level 3
know your network

Everyone everywhere is telling us we live in the new networked economy. We hear the words connectivity, wired world, global village and think, maybe I should be out there, part of it. But what is networking anyway and why is it so important to the float process?

Networking is nothing new. When Socrates stood in the square in Athens disseminating his wisdom or Queen Elizabeth I rallied support from her troops to gain control, they were networking with intent. You too need to understand how to build and manage your network so that you too maximize your value in the market. Ask any journalist how they get the breaking news; any senior manager how they got promoted; any company looking for new funds; any musician trying to land a record deal and they will generally say the same thing, they made contact through someone they knew.

This raises questions about cronyism and unfair advantage, as the individual excluded for whatever reason from the most powerful networks is sure to miss out on some benefits. Some realistic advice might be, if you really want the benefits offered by membership of one particular network, then find a way into it. This may not be perfectly fair, but we imperfect humans tend to associate with others of similar experience, background, or profession on the basis of comfort as well as enlightened self-interest.

For those of us who squirm at the very thought of networking
First things first, though. What does the idea of networking mean? Is it ethical? What behaviour lies within the boundary of friendship, what becomes a business relationship? How do we maintain relationships with integrity as well as pursue a commercial proposition? How do we network anyway? In the knowledge era, relationships and knowledge transfer are paramount. Your network is an ever-changing combination of friends and work colleagues and customers and suppliers. And the service era rulebook of boss and subordinate has changed, become informal. You can have a drink with your team without always doing the company line reinforcement act. Plus side: you have more network mobility. Minus side: you don't know if that is a benefit or not. What is the appropriate rulebook for this newly unhierarchical environment?

Coming back to your float, how do you feel you rate as skilled networker? Not great? Few of us are. Even the word itself seems a bit tainted, conjures up images of Mr Cheese the timeshare pyramid salesman and his unsavory 'you know I care' sales techniques. Squirm.

This is exactly why it is important to distinguish between cynical short-term networking, which is the same as aggressive selling, and networking with integrity, which aims to build mutually supportive relationships. So knowing yourself, and your value, is really important before you know your network level. Because here we are going to ask you, 'what are you networking to achieve? Because from that, relationships and content can more easily be worked out.

Learning how to build an integrity-rich network is an essential part of your float process.

Your ability to network is in effect a market multiplier. It takes your personal capital value of one and multiplies it by factors of 2-, 20- and possibly 200-hundred fold. This is because each person you know has their own network, and when there is real shared benefit and trust you potentially open the door to a range of new markets, simply by becoming an effective networker.

You create the network multiplier. If you choose to have a network of three people, then don't expect much of a compound value in the market. If, however, you can hit the magic figure of 100, that is 100 people who know your value and are helping you to promote it in the market. Your message will be in front of 100 people multiplied by their personal networks – which could be a vast number of people. Again, remember this is not just about selling. If you plan to become the best piano player in the world you are going to have to find the best tutor, and a sponsor – and your ability to network effectively is going to be critical.

Good networking accelerates your float process. Trade is a social act. Networking is a conscious decision to manage the social factors in your float process rather than perhaps letting them manage you.

Let's look back at where we are in the float levels.

Level 1. You know yourself and have a clear understanding of the float you wish to make, where it fits in with your life and the lives of those around you.

Level 2. You have managed to define the value of the float and how it might be applied in the market.

These first two are internal, i.e. you can do them on your own. So this is where the float testing begins. At the know your network stage, you will start to talk about your float idea. You will need to generate interest, to get people excited enough for them to tell other people about your great new ideas. This might be the end of it. You might see nothing but incredulity in the eyes of your first audience, pack up and go home. At this stage you will know if you have done enough work at levels 1 and 2, because if you have not, at the know your network stage any float flaws will become painfully apparent. Have you valued correctly? Is this really you? The know your network level can be a market amplifier, but it can also be a market silencer. If your network contacts don't believe that your ideas have value, they won't spread the word, your market entry will cease to exist and turn the light off as you leave, please. If you are lucky, your network will tell you why.

Let's consider someone who wants to float himself or herself within an organization. Martin wants to get promoted within his current firm. The reality is that any promotion is often a sign of trust. Now, would you trust someone you didn't know? Would you go on holiday and leave your home in possession of someone you hardly ever meet? You would insist on proof that this person will not damage or erode the value of your asset while you are away. In the same way, for Martin to get promoted he must help senior levels of the business understand his track record of achievement which should help them believe that promotion will increase, not erode, value creation within the business. He will do this via the process of conversation, talking to others who might have influence over the decision. All Martin is doing is offering those who manage the asset a chance to get to know him. And hopefully communicating the enhanced contribution he can bring to the business at the next level of management.

So value needs to be visible to be rewarded. An unseen drawing by Picasso locked in a safe somewhere is undervalued. Likewise, what is the point of knowing your own value, if you never take the time to convey any of the good news to people who might wish to make use of it?

Signpost

Good networking is where you:

- **Activate the abundance.** Good networking is a process grounded in integrity, working within areas of shared interest where all players benefit. There are clear steps to make this happen.

- **Build a bridge.** You can easily categorise your different relationships in the form of a relationship bridge to quickly gauge your level of interaction. The bridge will indicate the strength of the relationships, ranging from active to interactive.

- **Chart the connections.** Take the time to explore the richness of your network. Your value will be more extensively realized when your network is mapped, measured and managed.

- **Dare to be different.** If your network is a mirror extension of who you are then why bother? Your network needs to be a picture of who you want to be.

- **Entrust each other.** The level of trust in your network is directly proportional to the quality and quantity of value that it will create. By creating a network link with someone, you are entrusting that persona with your brand, market value and personal reputation. This is not something to be given lightly.

- ◆ **Fuel the flow.** People will always be part of more than one network, so you need to seek to refresh and re-energize your network such that it stays attractive to others. Any system in this universe has a natural tendency to entropy, and networks need maintenance work! You fuel the flow not just to maintain the network but to maintain and grow the level and value of human connectivity.

Activate your abundance

Personal capital is just that – it is the value that you have, own and are able to take to market.

However, if you have a scarcity mentality and treat it as something to hide and hoard it will never grow beyond its current size. If you develop an abundance mentality and give and take skills knowledge, network contacts, etc., you will allow your capital to keep developing in value and intrinsic benefit.

One example where social capital can be seen to be used to good effect is in Silicon Valley in California. Here social capital exists in the collaborative partnerships that emerged from the pursuit of innovation and technology market competitiveness. Countless collaborations sprang up to maximize on the networking and social capital potential.

In the same way as the Silicon Valley network, once your float network is in place you can expect to realize a number of significant benefits:

◆ **Market multiplier.** You access a larger market without having to incur huge sales and marketing costs. You can take option (a) spending days trying to speak to the decision maker, talking with the wrong people, in the wrong departments, meeting people who only want to have coffee because they are being made redundant and have nothing else to do. Or option (b) tap into a colleague's knowledge base and discover the major players, ensuring sales and marketing activities are more focused on the right person. Which sounds best to you? Neither? Ok. Well, moving on …

- **Market data.** You will often be able to gather and access data information that is not available in the open market. Friendly conversations provide more up-to-date knowledge than the financial pages.

- **Reduced cost.** A strong personal network will generally reduce the cost of checking and measurement within your float process. If you assume that any social network is founded upon the idea of shared values, goals and trust, then the need for formal contractual links is reduced and often eradicated. Say your float dream is to leave your current company and start up a small business selling handmade shoes and leather accessories. You'll need a good quality brochure. So you look for a good printer. Even when you find a printer, you'll spend valuable time checking to ensure that the final product is what you wanted. However, if you are able to tap into your network and find someone to produce your brochure, the cost may not be less, but there is a chance that they will have an understanding of your business needs and deliver a more suitable service. (If you start a small business selling shoes is it true that you are called a sole trader? Just a thought.)

- **Intangible value.** If I can create a network that is full of people who want to grow, then by virtue of my association there is every chance that I will grow almost without thinking. So, whenever I present myself to the market, part of that market representation is probably an element of my social capital or the value I have in partnership with others. Often this value is vague and intangible, but nevertheless it is real value. This is why people often choose carefully what university they will attend. It might not be just the quality of the lecturers, but often the quality of the students who will also be at the university.

As the old adage goes, it is not what you know, it is who you know that counts. It is such a measure that starts to put value on the worth of your social capital. This is why it is so important that you identify what are often unconscious decisions and move them to a conscious level. That way you can become more objective and selective about the types of relationship in your network.

Levels of social capital

To this end, it is wise to consciously measure the value that each relationship is adding against a simple template. And yes, this does seem strange – like many aspects of Float You we are taking you outside your comfort zone. Why? Because that is necessary for some perspective on your life, which you need in order to improve. Ok?

The notion of value creation is seen from a double perspective. To what extent are you creating social capital by association with the other person? And to what extent are they gaining value by association with you? To what extent are you jointly creating abundant value that emerges as a result of the social capital between you?

It is possible to map the nature of your relationship with different people against five value-based criteria seen in Fig. 9.1:

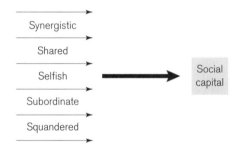

Figure 9.1 *Social capital levels*

1 **Squandered.** In this relationship little is happening. You might have links in place and invest time in each other, but the end result is that neither person is incurring any capital growth. You might send each other the occasional e-mail to say hello, but there is little activity on either side to grow the personal or social capital.

2 **Subordinate.** In this relationship value is being created, but you are not getting any of it. Your value creation is subordinate to that of the other person. The focus is on their getting benefit from you. You will only do this for a while unless you've decided on a new career as a doormat.

3 **Selfish.** This is the inverse of the subordinate level, where you do the taking, without giving anything back to them. Your personal capital is being multiplied by use of the network link, but it isn't

renewable and sustainable because the other person will eventually have enough of your demands and exploitation. (Unless they too are doormat wannabes.)

4 **Shared.** At this level, you are both gaining value from the relationship, but it is additive in nature. So there is little or no synergy between you. This might be seen in the case of the bricklayer and carpenter who work together. They do not offer new products or special discount schemes. They don't differentiate themselves in the market. They just work together and bill as if they were separate individuals. They have taken their value to market, but the social relationship is not acting as a multiplier on their personal capital.

5 **Synergistic.** This is a really important part of the idea of shared success. The most effective network relationship is where a number of people want to share ideas, collaborate to develop them and collectively create an answer. The net result is a compound or synergistic relationship, when the sum of the parts is greater than the whole. This is such a simple idea, often overlooked. Most people wouldn't even consider investing in a savings account where the end of year return was the same money returned plus a cost of living increase. We expect the bank to invest our money wisely into the market and to return interest on a compound basis. In the same way, if we plan to invest our float idea in the social market, we need to ensure that it is multiplied through association with others, and not eroded in value as it circulates.

Name	Social capital
1	
2	
3	
4	
5	
6	
7	
8	
9	
10	

Without thinking (much) write down the first 10 names of the people who you would count as being in your float network. Now, against each one write where they would fit on the value table.

Think about the resulting chart. To what extent is your personal network going to multiply the value of your float idea? Can you identify people who could drain your energy and potentially block your float? Are there people who give you helpful time and energy right now, but get little in return? Are there people who can take your float idea further than it is at the moment?

Do you feel you have created your network of ten through conscious choice, or has it evolved through happenstance? Did you even know that there was a word like happenstance? These semi-conscious moments of learning can pop up anywhere!

The point is that your network is a choice thing. And one that very few us take advantage of. This is a choice that you need to make as failure to truly realize abundance in your network means that you are failing to take all your float value to market.

Dilemmas of social capital

Hopefully we've established that networks will help the float and that managing them is a good thing to do, but there is one problem. What if the person you most need to network with is a real bigot? Or is there someone you really dislike who is crucial to the progress of the float? Well, the problem is that we don't have an answer. All we can do is draw you a nice box that might help you to make sense of the decision and how far you will go to make a float in your life.

Let us consider two key factors here. The first dimensions are the extent to which you like someone and the second is the extent to which you respect them. Put these together and you end up with the Like–Respect (LR) Map shown in Fig. 9.2.

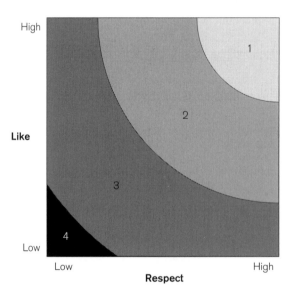

Figure 9.2 *LR Map*

This is a framework in which you can consider the membership of your network. It is all about what you will choose to do to achieve your float outcome.

Do you intend to operate at level 1, where you will only ever network with people you both respect and like? Are you prepared to operate at level 2, and be prepared to compromise a little? Maybe you are happy to run at level 3 and network with people you don't respect or like very much. Maybe you say, what the heck, and work at level 4 where anyone can be in your network long as they help you achieve what you want to achieve.

Maybe your model has a totally different shape, whereby the key criteria for you are respect and experience – and the liking bit doesn't come into it. Or, you have to like someone to be able to work with them but you are not really fussed about respecting them, just so long as they are fun to be with. Only you can decide, but we suggest that knowing the membership criteria of your float network is important, as you start learning how to build it.

Build a bridge

Progress check. You have defined some or all of your network, who you need to build and maintain links with. You are getting to grips with membership criteria. Now let's look at the nature of the relationship. Is it highly social, where you interact on a regular if not daily basis? Or inactive, a motionless relationship with little real warmth?

It is possible to categorize your different relationships in the form of a relationship bridge, to quickly gauge your level of interaction. This bridge has two sides. On the left-hand side is the relationship that you might define as inactive. You have a link with the person, but not much more. On the other side of the bridge is the interactive link, one where the strength of the relationship is just as important as any commercial or practical benefit gained from knowing or working with the person.

Active

Reactive   Proactive

Inactive   Interactive

Figure 9.3 Engagement bridge

◆ **Inactive.** Although the network relationship is in place, there is little activity taking place and nothing planned for the foreseeable future.

◆ **Reactive** Nothing much is in place although either of you might respond if the other person made the first move.

◆ **Active.** You are in contact with the person but nothing is really planned to occur. It is more one of those 'see you some time' type of relationships that has intent but little follow-through.

◆ **Proactive.** You have or are about to initiate a contact with the person and take such initiative on a regular basis. Contact is on a project-by-project basis. It is not a relationship where you would engage and interact with the person even if you did not have a project in place.

◆ **Interactive.** At this stage you have a natural ongoing relationship with the person sitting outside any planned project or action. You always keep in touch and do not wait for the other person to initiate the call. In this type of relationship there will normally be a date in the diary marking the next time you are going to meet or call the person.

Now think about your float process and take the 10 names that you listed on page 124 in the 'Activate your abundance' section and list them in the table below. When you have done that, allocate the nature of the relationship ranging from inactive to interactive.

Relationship	Inactive	Reactive	Active	Proactive	Interactive
1					
2					
3					
4					
5					
6					
7					
8					
9					
10					

Now ask yourself some questions:

- Do I have enough people in the interactive part to make the float happen?
- Where is the primary cluster or grouping of people in my network?
- Am I a good socializer or do I need to improve my ability to build social relationships?
- What should the spread of people be across the engagement bridge?
- What is the cost of maintaining people at the different points on the bridge?
- Are there people who I should let go of and take out of the network?

These questions indicate some of the choices you need to make as you start to chart the nature and construction of your float network.

Chart the connections

Lisa the networker. A salutary tale

Lisa is consolidating the big win of a large corporate client account. She is concentrating on managing the new business and taking care to integrate the new team. Her company has trebled its workload, and potential revenues, and Lisa is worried about having enough cover. She decides to call a few other firms that she knows to set up some informal chats and see if anyone is planning to leave who might want some freelance work with her.

Now Lisa, being an open sort of person, probably thought that a chat about life and a 'how much do you earn where you work?' sort of pitch was a bit cheeky, but morally ok. She felt that if they weren't happy they'd leave to go somewhere, and with web designers being in such short supply, why not let them know they'd be welcome to freelance on projects at her firm?

The day after one such informal chat, Lisa gets a call. The guy is pretty angry. She doesn't have any right to poach his people and he also warned the other local firms about her. 'So don't go asking favours from us again.' Lisa is really upset. Not thinking through the full implications of her networking has cost her a lot of friendly industry colleagues and possibly damaged her reputation as a person of integrity – for good.

Let's think about something nearer home. Your float. The goal that means most to you personally.

Chances are the float goal is exciting. You'll want everyone to know about it. Actually the temptation can be to rush out and network like crazy. You want to build a coalition of support, fast as possible. Right? Wrong. This would be comparable to a novice sailor buying a boat and setting sail across the Atlantic without any preparation. The nature of your float network is a critical decision. Consider the implications before you start to press the flesh.

Now you have started to chart two key factors that define the net value of your network. Just as a reminder, these are, (a) the level of social capital or value in each relationship and (b) how close you are. Consequently you can pull them together to start the process of charting the total value of the connections in your float network. This is shown in the *Net*Chart below. Each of the 30 points on the *Net*Chart indicates a particular form of relationship that can be found in any float network. This ranges from low value relationships to high value relationships.

	Inactive	Reactive	Active	Proactive	Interactive
Synergy		**Carrie**			**Dawn**
Shared					
Selfish					
Subordinate		**Bob**			
Squandered	**Alan**				**Eddie**

Activate abundance (vertical axis) — *Build bridges* (horizontal axis)

Figure 9.4 *Net*Chart

The *Net*Chart is used as a quick but powerful tool to help you chart the nature of your network, where value is being generated and what work you might need to undertake to enhance the success of your personal float. Ultimately it attempts to measure the value of your social capital and how it might help you to achieve the flotation.

In Fig. 9.4, five people have been considered who might be part of Martin's float network:

◆ **Alan** This is a network relationship that is going nowhere. There is little or no contact and when meetings do take place, they tend to be squandered with little or no value generation. The question might be why is the person still in Martin's network? If there is value to be generated from the association then he really could act to move the engagement forward, at least to active or proactive level. From this to try Martin can develop some shared or synergistic value. If Martin knows that this is unlikely to happen, perhaps it is time to pull the plug and let go of the relationship.

◆ **Bob** Martin meets Bob occasionally, but it is generally instigated when Bob needs a favour. The question again is should the relationship be maintained? Is there a way that Martin can equalize things? If so, he has to become more appropriately selfish. He is going to have to, if he wants the working relationship with Bob to get across the engagement bridge to a place of shared success.

◆ **Carrie** Martin's friendship with Carrie is interesting. They give each other a call once in a while, have lunch and both come up with great ideas for new companies, or plans to buy rental property together. Whenever they meet, they create value, but for some reason never quite move to the next logical stage of active or proactive. What prevents it? Perhaps Carrie got burned in the past in a business venture with a friend. Perhaps Martin is more cautious financially but talks up a good entrepreneurial future! Whatever the barrier, it will benefit both of them to make a move over the engagement bridge and at least get to the proactive level where they can aspire to eventually reach an interactive stage.

◆ **Dawn** The relationship with Dawn looks great. They are interactive, i.e. constantly in touch, and whenever they meet something new is created for both of them. The effort here might be to look into the future and ensure that there is some maintenance and TLC put in by both parties to keep things good.

◆ **Eddie** The relationship with Eddie is more difficult. There is clearly a strong link as they are both in contact and interactive, but whenever they meet there is little gain to be found. While such a social relationship can be fun, and Martin wants to make sure that the friendship stays in good shape, in terms of a useful player in his float network, time with Eddie has little value. A tough call has to be made – to either work hard and start to find ways to realize value, or move Eddie out of the float network but still hold on to her as a friend.

One of the key messages from the charting process is that YOU have to make choices about the shape and form of your network. You have to make decisions about the type of relationship and the value being created. Maybe you have to manage people out of the network where there is little current or future value to be realized. Maybe you have to define friends that can help you become all you want to be and friends that can't – but you love them anyway. The social network may be quite different to your float network. It's ok to distinguish. In fact the more clarity you can bring to the network, the better. Being clear with members of your network also shows respect.

Thinking about people that you know well or less well and deciding to evaluate them in terms of your float may feel like cold clinical stuff. And guess what – it is. Float networking is about making your float idea work; it is not just about making lots of great friends who you can party with. You can still have a social network where you have lots of fun, just try to ensure that you know the consequence of time in either network. On the doom and gloom side, this is a vital level of your route to market, or road to personal change. Know your network or potentially crash if you link with the wrong people, invest time in the wrong relationship or fail to take squandered relationships up to the synergistic level. Grown up stuff.

We're still working on it.

Time charting

Once you have the *Net*Chart in place, you can use this as a vehicle to map the nature of the relationships as they change over time. For example the *Net*Chart in Fig. 9.5 charts how the relationship changed as we (Carmel and Mick) met and developed the Float-You ideas.

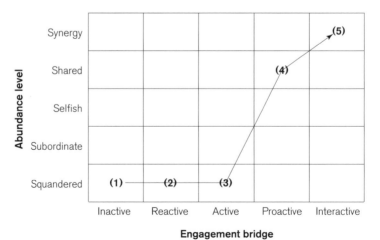

Figure 9.5 *Time NetChart*

Point (1) is when we first meet at a small consultancy firm in April 1999. Although we recognized the benefits that could grow from working together, for some reason we failed to build a working relationship and for a time, squandered the chance to generate value together. Over the following six months we moved through points (2) and (3) as we talked more and more about working together but never actually did anything. Finally around January 2000, we were talking about our beliefs and hopes when the idea of Float-You crystallized. We then swapped ideas and thoughts of how such an idea might work. This took us nicely to point (4) on the *Net*Chart. Finally, as we started to write the book, in April 2000, we were fair and square in position (5). Now, every time we meet something new seems to emerge and we interact quite naturally without any real need to prompt or push each other. (I push you lots. Who wrote that?)

Finally, don't assume that all your links need to be at the interactive level. Accept that your network is dynamic and relationships change. Don't attempt to over-regulate or control because ultimately, in the modern economy, links that are too permanent might actually fuel the collapse of the network. In a purely commercial sense, your network needs to flex and adapt at a speed that exceeds the rate of change of the industry where it resides.

Dare to be different

Your network is the best distribution channel you will ever have. So if you want your network to sponsor you and your float ideas, they need to know what they are promoting and how it differs from everything else in their network.

As with any product, the brand built around your idea will influence the degree of interest in it. You'll want to think your float idea is different, sexy, and all the rest. To other people your idea is another cornflake packet in the long row of cornflake packets in the supermarket. There are lots of good ideas out there. So a really big question is how to create large amounts of interest in your float. What will make people listen to you rather than to anyone else's float proposition?

As with any product, the brand built around your idea will influence the degree of interest in it.

Try to sit back a bit from your float idea. How would you simplify the main concepts? How would you convey those to other people? Clarify the essence, and condense your personal float into around 25 words. At first try you'll need more words. Keep whittling and don't lose the rich essence of your float and how special it is. If after quite a few attempts it still isn't possible to summarize at 25 words, don't bother. If you can't keep it down to 25 words, no matter how good it is, if you can't describe it as you are walking with someone between meetings, then there is little chance that anyone will ever get the time to listen. Yes that is tough. You get 30 seconds airtime for your 'elevator pitch', if that, so the float needs to live in your head as a great soundbite. To help you summarize, here is an exercise. Any good brand description has to meet at least four key criteria, as seen in Fig. 9.6:

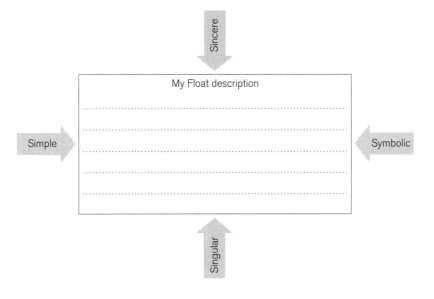

Figure 9.6 *Float description*

Simple

Can you keep the idea so simple that you could get the message across to someone in a crowded bar, over a couple of sips of beer. Look at any effective brand in the market and in most cases there is something memorable and very simple. This takes one of two forms. A logo (see Symbolic below). Or a strapline 'always Coca Cola' or 'Gillette – the best a man can get'. They are both straightforward and easily replicable so they can be communicated and copied with ease.

◆ Can you describe the float idea in a few words?

◆ When you wake up in the morning does it spring into your thinking (even with a hangover)?

◆ Could you describe it to a group of children so they understand?

◆ Is it free of jargon, long words or abbreviations?

Singular

It needs to appear to be unique – even if you are adapting an existing idea, it needs spin to make it appear unique in the market. Brand recognition needs to be instantaneous. The Red Cross symbol for medical care is unique and generally recognized across the world.

Can you generate a simple and unique identity that your network will associate with you and no one else?

◆ When you describe it does it remind you of anything?

◆ If you told a neighbour have they said, 'oh that reminds me of'?

◆ If you scan the web using your key float words, does anything come up?

Sincere
People know when someone is faking it, so always ensure that your brand positioning description is true to your beliefs and values. If it is not authentic you risk looking a bit stupid to those who really know you!

◆ When the float idea is written down, does it feel comfortable to you?

◆ When you describe it to others, is there some incredulity, or do they light up and say that it sounds just like you?

◆ If you had a choice between this float and other options, would you still pick it?

Symbolic
It can really help to have a symbol that represents your float idea. For example, in 1971, Carolyn Davidson was paid $35 to design a logo for a small Oregon sports shoe company. The result was the world famous Nike brand logo of the tick. The emblem was built around the idea of speed and movement, which led to the 'swoosh' which emphasizes the essence of Nike sports products.

◆ When you describe the float, what feelings does it evoke in others?

◆ Can you reframe it in the form of a parable or fairy story?

◆ How would you draw it on the back of an envelope?

Imagine that you are sitting in a coffee bar and overhear one of your network members describing you to another person – are you happy with the way they describe your float idea? If not then it suggests that you have failed to build and communicate your float brand effectively.

Entrust each other

Ok, so you have a network in place, you have started to share your young brand float idea with them. There is another area to consider: trust. Why should they trust you? OK, they know you and you seem like a good person, but they really won't entrust their personal capital if there is any risk that you might corrupt or undermine their value in the market. The only reason why they will invest their time, energy and brand is if they trust you.

Your float will have to be sold as an idea, even if it is not about commercial gain. If you want to find new sponsors for a local charity scheme, you still need to sell. So your desire to create a network with people is in some ways similar to any salesperson. And you may well feel the cold chill of rejection from those you wish to engage. It isn't personal, people just don't have time to do everything. They may need some persuasion, so developing a float network can be like a sales process. And as any top salesperson will tell you, the fuel for sales is trust. So this next section considers how you build a robust and valuable network by establishing more trust-based relationships. First of all, a few network principles:

- ◆ Networks are about the exchange of information.

- ◆ This exchange is based upon a core ability to trust the other person with your resources and reputation.

- ◆ Trust doesn't just happen – it has to be created in partnership as both sides invest time, energy and emotion in each other.

- ◆ This means you need to invest in, or entrust yourself to, the other person before you can expect them to trust you.

- ◆ As both partners in the network invest in the trust fund so it will act as a compound investment and grow of its own accord.

◆ as a result the level of trust in your network is directly proportional to the quality and quantity of value that it will create.

Your trustability index
As this is a key aspect of networking, ask yourself these questions:

◆ To what extent do you act in a trustworthy manner? For example,

  – Do you reschedule people with little notice if something better comes up?

  – Do you exaggerate stories to make yourself look good?

  – Do you break promises?

◆ What do you look for in others before you trust them?

◆ How do you measure the level of trust in a network?

◆ What action can you take to enhance the level of trust in a relationship?

◆ How can you build connections based upon real trust and operate at a deeper than surface or superficial level?

In your personal life trust is often an unspoken given that is assumed to happen. In your float network, trust really should be managed. Consciously, with passion and integrity. This way is also emotionally and spiritually fulfilling – you are building a float community which will give you strength and support just by existing.

A successful and sustainable network will grow from your empathy and trust. Because trust is the oil that lubricates the process of building close and effective network relationships.

Trust funds

As you define and chart your network, you decide to invest time, money and energy in another person on the basis that there will be some form of payback. Not meant cynically. Payback might be a chance to express your generosity through supporting a friend in need. Your investment might be taking the time to write to them, go for a drink, listen to their problems or explain how your float idea is going to work. By doing this you are making the deliberate choice to 'not' invest your personal resource in someone else on the basis that their contribution to your float might be less.

Whoa – 'what a cold uncaring schemer' we hear you say – 'you can't treat people in the same way that you treat bank accounts and investment funds'. Oh yes you can! This doesn't negate the love and care and trust and support side. That, in fact, will be more present because you network less with people you don't like or respect.

Paula's network plan

Paula has really worked this one out. To remind you, she recently completed an adult literacy programme and started a pre-university entry course. She wants to study conservation management and get a job working in forestry. She has come a long way already and is becoming more confident that she can make things happen. In her words, 'My social relationship with my friends and family is just that, a social network that has nothing to do with my studies. On my entry course I have found some very helpful tutors and they are encouraging me to talk to universities already about getting onto a programme next year. I want to get as many forestry contacts as I can and make sure that I stand out as someone trustworthy and dependable, because they get a lot of applications. Creating that impression is down to me.'

How can you define trust? If you accept that good relationships are founded upon trust; then you need to take hold of this vague thing and make it manageable and measurable.

Float candidates (with you perhaps in that category) therefore invest in their relationships with other people as well as their float idea. Without a float network out there telling the world, your float is going to be a long time coming.

Fuel the flow

The trust-based relationships which make up your network will need some TLC if they are to stay valuable, and you'll need to invest time to help fuel your network's growth and help it to survive. What does that mean? It means these things:

◆ maintenance routines

◆ keeping an eye on the market to ensure other potentially competing networks don't become more attractive to your network members

◆ making sure you don't drain the value from the network like a greedy fisherman who harvests too many fish from a lake.

This is probably new stuff to you, so here are some simple guidelines on how to make it happen.

Pulse, pulse and pulse again

Take every opportunity to pulse the network to keep it live and enthused. The people in your networks have other jobs, interests and links into other networks. Consciously do things to stay in front of their mind. It is easy to forget someone when you have a lot on your plate – don't take it personally! Make sure you have a process in place to pulse the network on a regular basis. Like a radar sweep rotates and touches every point on the horizon in a pattern, it helps if you can define the sweep pattern that you will use to maintain your network.

This is not to suggest a mechanical, automated process to just pump out the latest 'hi and how are you' message. The idea is to set up triggers to ensure that you do not forget or lose track of valuable members of the network. Pulsing simply ensures the contact is open and relationships maintained. So when opportunities do come along you are both emotionally and intellectually ready to create new synergies in the market.

This might be by personally checking out with people how they are and what they are involved in; setting up a newsletter to send out on a regular basis to keep people informed of your ideas; responding to other people's newsletters to comment on their ideas or float products; letting the network know of any specific news items that catch your eye and might be of interest to them. Choose one that feels authentic to you. If you are more introverted, you may prefer to telephone rather than attend social events. If you are an extrovert typing a newsletter may be much less fun than going over for coffee and a catch-up. No matter what you do, regular pulsing will ensure your float idea stays to the front of people's minds.

Don't be greedy

As a good fisherman will cast back the small fish to conserve and create stocks for the future, so the good networker will not abuse their network stock of goodwill. Consider the network like a common resource, abuse of any open or common resource has the same consequences. This concept applied to land, for example, is known as the 'tragedy of the commons', referring to overuse and destruction of shared land resources. Shared land can be depleted when shepherds each pursue a selfish interest (and graze their sheep presumably) without regard for their peers or the land.

In the context of a network, consider that what feels right to you, e.g. sending out a newsletter, setting up meetings, multiplied by each network member, ends up as overbearing and possibly draining for each network member. Instead of valued update, it starts to look like junk mail. Your float update – groan. Delete. You need to see yourself in context. And be sensitive to the medium and the message.

So, how to overcome this potential problem? It starts with you. Recognize your network is a shared resource and consider the most appropriate and caring approach to pulse and pulse again. It really will be worth it.

Separate float from friends

One of the most difficult aspects of any network is how to separate out the personal network from the float network. This can be quite a difficult call to make. You are going to find times when you want help from friends with your float and vice versa. And work colleagues start to become friends. Although this will always happen, the sustainability of the float network is often dependent on your ability to take on dual roles. To separate out two sides of yourself. One day you might be talking to someone about a new commercial product as part of your float and how you might share commission. Later on you both share a social evening.

You want to keep both aspects distinct and avoid any potential conflict in one overspilling into the other. Be prepared to openly recognize and talk about the two relationships and manage them in different ways. If you try to manage them differently without sharing why you are doing so with the other person then at best you cause confusion, at worse you come across as duplicitous and unprofessional. So take care on this, ok?

level 4
know your market

You couldn't exist with only one breath. Likewise, achieving your float outcome will take more than one marketing push, or even two or three. You keep breathing and stay alive. To ensure that your float is on track you are going learn how to market your own unique float proposition. Then keep marketing day in and day out. Every part of your float is dependent upon one person – you. Marketing traditionally uses the four ps – product, price, promotion and placement. We are going to consider your float with a marketing mindset. You may even find this is where you decide to buy yourself!

Signpost

To know your market you must:

◆ **Sell the sizzle.** Understand the how your float product can survive and prosper in a world of imitation, replication and global copying. Understand and market the float essence, the benefits, the unique wraparound from your float. There is a phrase for this: 'sell the sizzle, not the steak' (or the crunchy coating, not the quorn fillet). Whatever does it for you!

◆ **Burn your brand.** Know how to burn your float brand into the mind of everyone who buys into your dream. People don't go out anymore to buy a pack of paper tissues or jeans – they go to buy

Kleenex or a pair of low-hip 501s. The question is, how can you make your float offering more attractive?

- **Map the market.** Create a detailed map to define the dynamics of the market you plan to enter. Be sure that the giant leap you plan to take with your float is not out-stepped by your competitor.

- **Niche your niche.** Take your level of differentiation to a niche level. Consider how to target a market that is so specialized that you can become the number one there, before others get a chance to enter.

- **Hit the hot spot.** Know how to make your float idea real for a million people. Use the tools of socialization and specialization to get yourself to market.

- **Market with meaning.** Understand how the tools of manifestos and mouth-to-mouth marketing will help Float-You. Float integrity, purpose and close, trust-based relationships – and that way ensure your float is sustainable and fulfilling.

Sell the sizzle

Your float is unique. It may be about personal challenge or growth. It may be launching a new business. This next part considers the need to retain ownership of your float value by assessing the potential threats. While this is most applicable to a commercial float, there are universal lessons.

Don't let yours be a ripped-off float
Many good ideas become physical objects, are taken to market and sold for a profit. Think about books, sheet music, records, newspapers, loose-leaf binders, tapes, discs, and other electronic media. Historically, however, it was hard to mass-produce and market information, it could only be re-implemented or transferred. Originals were copied, people passed on wisdom or techniques. Re-implementation was cumbersome and re-use did not take away from the original, but creating the means of implementation – a new machine or a trained apprentice – took considerable time and physical resources. It also incurred significant cost to anyone who wanted to copy the original intellectual property.

However, with the growth of web-based services, cheap technology and low cost overseas workforces, it is relatively easy to copy intellectual property. It isn't right, but it is widespread. Assuming there is an information element of your float idea, there is a chance that someone somewhere will be able to copy it. Once copied they can pass it off as their original, and take the value from your potential market. So consider your level of control over your float idea. Can it fall prey to others copying and passing on your property?

This poses a challenge. What extent of your float content can be copied and replicated? How will you receive compensation for your float if part of it can be replicated without your control? What should the float candidate do? Perhaps turn the problem on its head and into an opportunity. Define what element of your intellectual property can be given away free in order to sell support services and build closer relationships. Your goal is to figure out what to charge for and what to give away – all in the context of what other providers are doing and what customers (will grow to) expect.

This is not to suggest that content is worthless, or that you have to give it away for free. You need to manage your idea as if it were free, and then be creative to consider how to set up relationships or develop support products and services that cover the costs of developing content. By giving something away, you will benefit. How? Like this:

◆ users provide feedback on the float product idea or service

◆ you improve based on feedback

◆ free word-of-mouth market share

◆ building relationships with people who may pay for other float offerings.

You may want to consider how to do this. The solution might be to:

◆ Control not the copies of your work but instead a relationship with the customers – subscriptions or membership, for example.

◆ Charge on a usage basis, with fees small enough that people can't be bothered to go to the inconvenience of copying your ideas.

◆ Sell upgrades rather than the initial product.

◆ Give the product free but use the marketing data to sell other products (ethically of course).

◆ Make the free service dependent on your personal support, so than no one else can copy the personal delivery.

◆ Give the idea away free and charge for training or local customization.

◆ Sell the opportunity for your customers to modify your idea at source and create something that is unique for them.

So identify what about your float idea is the sizzle, then consider how that can develop perhaps taking some of the ideas shown above (giving stuff away for free!).

High market value comes from the float that touches other people's lives. Your float needs to come across as personally relevant, trusted, unique, branded and support service focused. The value of your float might well be in the surround factors rather than the actual float itself.

Burn your brand

Ok, some of us are brand lovers, some of us not. They undoubtedly work for a lot of people. So how can you brand your unique float idea so that it is in the hearts and at the front of the minds of potential buyers? If your float is there, you have probably influenced behaviour. Heart leads to head, which leads to hand which potentially leads to market revenue.

The brand journey is a complex one. There are some key brand factors to consider if you are to take your float to market and help it stick. They are:

- the creation of a brand that is trusted to be part of the family

- how to create a sense of 'customer stickiness' in the brand

- building a flexible brand position, with the future in mind

- ensuring that the branding is true to you, your value and your float dream.

Brand definition: Recognizable symbol or summary of trusted service or product. It is something that creates instant consumer recognition in the market.

Some brands are cool by association. The test of any brand is whether people are proud to be associated with your idea. Successful branding is about emotional engagement at individual level. Disney can sell a million theme park tickets for 'the magical kingdom'. Amazon.com has over 19 million regular customers, many of whom

your float strategy

float you

momentum

click on the site even when they are not planning to buy. The brand is not a business case. It is not a social appeal to goodness. It reinforces the buyer's identity. Remember the heart to head to hand link.

Now, what is it about your float idea that goes straight to the heart? Wow, I want some of that! When you talk about your goal does it create excitement – for you and the person you are talking to? How can you create an experience around your float proposition?

Lisa's delivery

Tough times since we last heard from Lisa. Her *faux pas* in trying to poach staff from a competitor firm has hit hard. She has lost confidence. The nagging voice telling her she could never hack it has grown in volume. She feels she has lost momentum. And now sales are dropping.

One morning, in the office, Lisa received of a bunch of flowers. Thank you from Marie. Marie was a good friend who had needed some financial help a year ago. Lisa had forgotten all about it.

Sitting there, feeling really touched by the gesture, Lisa realized the thing she was most upset about was feeling her naïve mistake had tarnished her personal reputation. She felt like a bad person. The flowers reminded her that she did have a nice side. And she realized that she had to get out there and recover the damage.

That evening Lisa dug out all the customer feedback she'd had. And then the kinds of things she would love other people to say about her firm. Both were surprisingly unrelated to good web design – that was the asking price to her market. It was more the way she and her team listened to the customer and conveyed the essence of their brand through her designs. For instance, she put an animated blue sea and ocean background on one travel agent's site. It looked realistic, sunny and warm – and traffic on the site increased as more people considered a plane ticket away from winter.

After talking these revelations through with the team, they realized this was an untapped brand advantage. They did much more than other web design firms – they understood the essence of their customer business and were able to translate that into great online marketing. The new strapline was

LG Web Design and Marketing Services: 'We help you reach out and touch your online customers'

Lisa phoned her friend to say thanks for the flowers and knew she was really grateful. Because she had reconnected her own fire inside. Back to work!

Just like Lisa, you have to identify and then burn your float brand into the heart and head of your audience. Remember, your competitors seek to do the same.

There is a balancing act to manage here. Your brand needs to be memorable, but also flexible and able to adapt to new market needs. Futureproof the brand by ensuring the message is current but universal. No point in being Britain's Favourite Millennium Mustard in 2012!

Finally, don't brand yourself at the expense of your values. Film producer Spike Lee is a leading social commentator in America. He said 'I know that people can be brands but I don't consider myself to be a brand. I think of myself as an artist. If I saw myself as a brand that could create a conflict and could damage my integrity.'

At the outset of your float development, clarify the values that drive you and your float brand. Hold on to these values dearly and don't ever let go. As your float proposition grows, check back on these to ensure that you stay true to your original beliefs. To thine own self be true – don't forget who you are for the sake of the commercial hit of groovy branding in the market.

Map the market

What does your float market look like? What did it look like last year and what will it be like next year? Is it a geographical audience, e.g. everyone in Yorkshire? Is it grown-up boys who buy electronic toys? How much business is transacted in that marketplace? What is 10 per cent market share worth?

By mapping your float against a time-based market position, you increase your competitor awareness and can feel sure you have targeted a sustainable market sector.

Let's consider Paul, a talented musician who also makes guitars for his friends. He has decided to leave his job as a barman to set up a business making instruments in a local workshop.

A friend of his has a similar business, going well. He is able to earn a good living and also have time to play in a band. Paul decides to tackle float level 1. He understands the difficult choices he needs to make, has a clear outcome in mind and has managed to get the support of all the stakeholders in his life. He then deals with float level 2 and ensures he has the necessary skills to design, make and market instruments. He believes that part of his strength in the market is his ability to make a guitar based upon an early design by Leo Defner. He can do this because he spent his early years working in the Defner factory, and was lucky enough to learn from some of the original master guitar makers.

Because he worked so closely with them he was able to understand many of their tacit skills. One of these was the unique way of allowing the wood to season just until it was ready to be formed into the core guitar. From float level 3 he took the time to socialize with his network of musician friends, making sure they know about his business building niche guitars. He manages to enlist their support to pass the word around.

All is looking good; he has the motivation, the skills and a solid network of people who will promote his niche guitars. So with his money in hand (a loan from the bank manager) he invests in a lathe, a batch of expensive wood, and a workshop. Although the cost has been quite high, he is convinced that his niche product is so specialized and in demand that he will soon be able to repay the loan and move into profit.

Two weeks later Paul opens the music press papers and notices an ad:

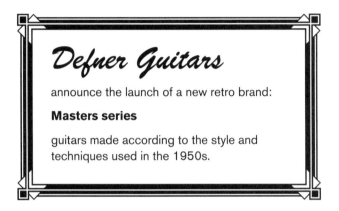

Defner Guitars

announce the launch of a new retro brand:

Masters series

guitars made according to the style and techniques used in the 1950s.

Bang – say goodbye to Paul's new business.

No matter how hard he works, and even though a few friends might buy guitars just because they are loyal to him, he will never be able to match the production rate and low costs achieved by a large multinational manufacturer. Paul's mistake was to view his float in isolation and not take time out to map the market in its entirety. His float has been out-floated by a competitor in the market.

It is all very well having a niche product in the high street, but it is only niche until someone else sells the same product in a different shop. If you are investing your time, energy and love into your float, you must expend the same amount of time and energy to understand the your float marketplace.

The market tide will also change. Sometimes it might increase and flood your area with competitors who out price you. Other times it might ebb away – the market grows tired of the punk rock band, 30in. flares, or specialist beer with a piece of fruit in the top. In flow or ebb, have a strategy to deal with market tides.

Consider the examples below of people who have fallen foul of changing market tides:

◆ The manager who has spent three years getting her Masters of Business Administration degree at night school only to find that the Doctorate of Business Administration is now the *de facto* standard in the market she wants to enter.

◆ The manager who retires after making enough money in the city to buy a fishing business in Cornwall only to find that the EC bans fishing in that area because of dangerously low stocks.

◆ The entrepreneur who decides to open a new wine bar in the high street only to find that three other bars are granted a licence in the same area, in the following week.

In all four cases the float candidate has not taken market tides seriously enough to understand how they could sweep their dream away in seconds. This problem is compounded when you consider that one small area of ocean can have a range of different tides floating through it. So for any float venture, take the time to gain perspective. Map the market to understand the cyclical nature that the tides follow and how they can impact upon you.

Let's take another example. Imagine you are a sales manager who decides to go for promotion. You might invest a lot more time improving your skills and keeping your network up.

Your team are about to put in place a new set of procedures and reward systems that will probably enhance the overall sales performance by 5 per cent a year. So, you work out that if you can increase your personal sales by 10 per cent you will rise above the team growth and stand out in the crowd and become more promotable. As seen in Fig. 9.6.

Figure 9.6 *Personal float performance increase*

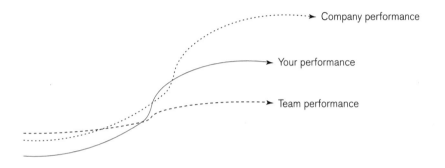

Figure 9.7 *Company float performance*

However, what you don't realize is that the company plans to float on the market in a year from now. To make the business attract a high level of investor interest, it plans to increase sales performance by 44 per cent. Unfortunately, being asset strippers at heart, they aim to achieve this by sacking anyone who does not achieve a 20 per cent growth target, and bringing in external sales professionals who can hit the targets. So you might spend all your time reaching for this 10 per cent goal only to find that factors outside your control kill your personal float.

You might be fast. Are you fast enough?

Niche your niche

Markets are big, damned big. Big markets include drinkers, TV audiences, readers. You! Big brands such as CNN or Levis or Coca-Cola have established pretty permanent access to a wide market. It has taken a long time and huge advertising spend (and, in the case of Coke, direct help from the US government!). So they are in a wonderful position.

If your float is to create a commercial product or service, you won't be able to go all out at the big markets. It is simply too expensive. The realistic option is to crack the market into small chunks or segments. This is niche marketing. One example: extract from those people who watch TV those people who watch TV at night, then those who watch TV at 4 am after they have been clubbing, then divide this segment again into an even smaller niche segment of gay people who watch TV after a night out clubbing. The late night gay audience is your niche, and one that is regularly targeted by firms advertising chat lines, holidays and gyms. Now for Coke there isn't really any need to specifically capture that audience. For your personal gym just getting started, it would be perfect. Just capture 2 per cent of that profitable niche and your float takes off.

This niche market is often attractive because customers located there have distinct and unique characteristics and needs. They are often prepared to pay a premium price for the right products or services. You understand these specialist needs and make sure your product meets demand.

If you get this right, your business will grow and start to achieve economies of scale. Then, guess what? Competition. Even more specialized and a bit cheaper. Most competitors are unwilling to go in because of your market dominance. The real kick starts when the mass market starts to recognize the value of your niche and you have the primary share of mind for this market as the leader in the field. Consider the growth of Anita Roddick's float idea of a shop selling green beauty products. The Body Shop started as a niche model, and grew as customers bought into the idea. It has now reached a stage where there are many green cosmetic products – built perhaps from ideas she took to market?

Part of our float niche strategy (along with many others) is to take our ideas and beliefs to the readership market through this book. However, we are amazed every time we walk into the office of our editor. Every day another batch of book proposals arrives on her desk, and this doesn't take into account the ideas and manuscripts sent in by e-mail, fax, or over the telephone. Each of these manuscripts or ideas is probably a float in some way or other for the author. They might be the end result of 20 years' part-time research or an outline idea dreamed up yesterday in a restaurant.

Whatever, the submission of the idea and manuscript is the moment where the author's float hits the market, and the publishing editor acts as the market filter with authority to accept or reject that idea.

Even when the editor accepts the idea (and you've stopped cartwheeling with joy around the office), the decision has to be sanctioned by an editorial review board that needs to be convinced of its commercial merits. The next market filter is the bookshop. Do they think the book will sell, and will they choose this over the other books being launched? The book makes it onto a bookstore shelf. Then the final market filter is probably you. Just why did you buy this book? (Thanks again, by the way.) What was your motivation to part with your hard earned money? Did the jacket appeal to you? Was it the title? Maybe the concept of floating? Maybe you have an interest in the financial market and the analogy between personal development and the financial markets caught your eye.

Why does any product make its way through so many gates or market filters? To take our own experience, we realize that although we both have a passionate desire to help others release their potential, so do many other people. Look in any bookshop and the personal development section is big and growing. Our niche strategy got us through the first market filter – our editor – through the float/IPO analogy. That and being such lovely folk and all. We

your float strategy

float you

momentum

suggested that this book would be of immense value to people who want to develop themselves in a way that helps them to optimize their personal capital in the market, be that commercial or achieving a great personal goal, like yours.

Niche the niche has universal application. We know we have mostly detailed the commercial side. Even if your float is simply becoming more assertive where you work, you will have to define the audience for your new assertiveness, as well as the exact nature of your newly assertive behaviour.

If your float is going to India to learn how to meditate, you will need to find an ashram and convince them that you are serious about your commitment and that means working out your kind of ashram and your uniquely committed reasons.

One last point. We just want to put in another integrity reminder. When you carve out your niche make sure it's an accurate projection of your true identity. If you are able to niche your niche in a way that creates goodwill and trust, then come competition or market tide you will have created brand loyalty. Often it is the tacit, deep values that are going to be the most important part of your personal brand. No one can replicate it. And it is true to the essence of you.

Whatever your strategy, make sure your niche is big enough to get a lot of customers from your territory, and small enough to eliminate any competitors. That's quite a challenge and a lot of work, but once you've done it, get ready to float big time.

As a small player, you are unlikely to have the market volume, clout and investment capability that other players in the market have. So if you can't enter the market on their terms, then just change the terms!

Hit the hot spot

How do you take your float into the hearts and minds of people who don't know you? There are two challenges: first, although you might deal with people you know socially, the odds are that at some stage you will have to move from an unknown or little known position. Second, how do you create demand for your float idea, rather than having to actively market and push? If you combine the four elements of the extent to which you are known or unknown, pushing your product or creating a pull in the market, you end up with the hot spot model shown in Fig. 9.8.

The aim here is to hit the hot spot. In the warm front or warm feelings quadrant, you have a market edge over those in the cold chill quadrant. (Bear with us on this. We haven't been overdosing on

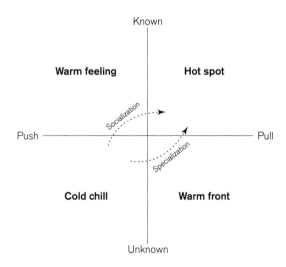

Figure 9.8 *Hot spot*

the weather channel!). People buy from or help those they know and trust. The question is, how can someone in the cold chill quadrant build relationships with people in the market who are interested in your float idea?

The first option is the common approach of socialization. For example, conferences, seminars, trade fairs. Even being involved with non-violent direct action events! This ability to get on a personal level with a potential buyer of your idea makes it much easier to form a working relationship.

The second option is to take the specialization route – to build a known brand in the market such that people value the skills or knowledge that you offer. Access to the market depends on people becoming aware of you. This means speaking publicly, writing a book, regular articles for a well known publication, or being on television. As a result, the customer decides that you offer a solution to their problem. One example is the political pundit. During each election campaign, the same old commentators keep reappearing because they are recognized authority figures. Niche TV guru status is all about credibility, presence, and – if you are female – always try to be young and beautiful as well as professional and experienced. Oh sorry, that's another tangent. (Just to finish this though – in float success terms, gender bias sometimes makes us wonder 'is it a girl or a buoyant'.)

Back to you. Your strategy belongs to you – what can you do to develop social relationships with your potential float backers? How can you ensure that your particular niche or specialism is seen in the market as attractive. Think about your float and add some ideas here.

My socialization strategies

My specialization strategies

Hitting the hot spot is just the beginning. You then need to develop a credible, convincing and close relationship with the client or float backer. One that helps them feel confident that you have something they want to buy. The socialization and specialist strategies will help you get through the front door, not into the customer's wallet.

Market with meaning

People no longer want to be seen as types – to fit into a category or to be pigeon-holed as a 'targeted type'. The old rules of marketing might not work in fast-changing, individualized society. Any potential customer or float backer needs to know the 'whole picture' that your float relates to. So your role as float marketer is to make it easy for them to understand what they are buying and why they are buying your idea. To create the all important 'aha' moment as they start to understand your unique offering.

But how to reach into this more selective marketplace? One way might be to evolve your float idea into a manifesto, a powerful statement, bringing existing ideas together, adding your unique analysis and thereby transforming them into a new, larger idea that's unified and compelling.

Manifesto marketing is based on the principle that we are shifting from broad-based markets with highly defined market segments to person-to-person marketing, where the unit of one is paramount. The need for a manifesto occurs because:

1 You don't market to markets – you market to people.

2 As products become more personal, so buyers want to buy from someone with a shared belief.

3 If you sell cheap, someone will always sell cheaper overnight.

4 If you market based on your unique beliefs, then there is less chance of replication of those beliefs.

5 Beliefs are shared and learnt through conversation – not bland commercials or slogans.

6 Markets are places where conversations and meaning are facilitated and aided by the marketer.

7 The web-enabled society is opening up channels of conversation around the world.

8 If you want to take a position in the market – you need to take a position – this position is represented in the form of a manifesto.

DIY manifesto kit

◆ In as few words as necessary, describe what your float is about, why it is important, who it is for and what will be different when the outcome is achieved.

◆ Accurately, honestly and entertainingly, introduce the foundations that support your float. Create a fertile meeting ground for discussion, debate and enlightened conversation.

◆ Get up close and personal: write the manifesto as though you are writing to a friend, not a market.

◆ Create a new language. Great ideas take the wisdom of the past and reframe it in a new language that makes sense for the future. Help to stimulate a new thread of conversation based upon your ideas, thoughts and beliefs.

◆ Share success with your reader; don't do it to the reader, try to create a sense of mutual gain where we both achieve our goals.

◆ Ensure that your values are apparent and obvious in the manifesto. Show commitment to those things that you are committed to.

◆ Debunk old myths and create new dreams. Any new community needs its own legitimate heroes and heroines, its models and mentors.

◆ Create conversations, stimulate debates, provoke arguments, create healthy tension. Offer the first – not the last – word in cutting-edge thinking.

level 5
now float

When someone asks, what does Float You look like, you might consider the following aspects.

Float You is about change, it creates something new
Float You is more than trying to fix something, whether that be your life, your company or even saving the world. Fixing something is not the same as creating something new. There is a big difference between making a change to make things better and creating a new option in your life. Float You creates something new.

Float You is an everyday experience – with some glorious breakthroughs
Because sometimes you just get those. But not to order – which might be a disappointment for those who wanted the final chapter of this book to be a tidal wave of personal insight. However, for the fans of the big splash, please don't rule it out. They may happen quite quietly.

The image is of a person bursting through a wall of water, emerging with a smile, energized, free. Liberated. Which is a nice image. But it may not be where you are now. You may not do heroic at this time in the morning. All the tools and techniques need one more critical ingredient: your action. 'Yeah ok. I'll think about it. Tomorrow, yeah?' No. The present moment is a very good time. Here and now you have all the things you need to start. Reading this, right now, 2 per cent of you are just around now deciding that you are going to go for it. Do you think you might be in that 2 per cent? Lots of action on the everyday scale will, like regular savings, compound your happier, 'floated' way of life.

Now Float. Imagine, living each moment with awareness, awareness of choice, of priorities. Able to tolerate high doses of pleasure, spare cash, love. Not able or willing to tolerate victimhood – whether that is self or external.

There are some words that we want to help you install. What do we mean, install? We mean put this software – float thinking – into your hardware, your head
The key is action. Action and then some more action. Activists frequently say that action brings hope. My own experience as a social activist has been that non-violent action affirmed my personal voice, my unique humanity. It also continues to give a fantastic opportunity to be mentally, spiritually, emotionally present during the years of my existence. Now do it.

Signpost

◆ **Give a damn.** Your float outcome will both cause and require a big heart. Float means optimize your personal capital which, for lasting happiness, better be bigger than cash. Lennon and McCartney sang 'Money can't buy me love.' Be a social crusader. Get passionate about your life instead of someone else's profit. In fact, something wider than anyone's profit. Open your heart. Plan to succeed with a social objective. Look for market solutions to social problems.

◆ **Live large.** Define your hopes and dreams without limits. See your float dreams coming true with joy and ease. Expect fun. Do something every day outside your comfort zone, even if it's just a new ice-cream flavour. Random acts of beauty and senseless acts of kindness.

◆ **Release the brake.** Taking your foot off the brake is as beneficial as pressing hard on the gas. The brake is fear. So the float isn't likely to be here anytime soon unless you deal with your fear.

◆ **Ask the question.** Float You helps you optimize your personal capital. But what if the float doesn't go well? Ask the question, do a worst case scenario. Asking better questions gives you better answers. You are going to float, and be fully prepared for whatever outcome – because you are able to ask the big questions.

◆ **Love it.** Ask any post-float individual how their life is going. This is the answer you'll get. I love it. Love it, see, taste, feel the pleasures of achievement, of being up there on a stage built with your own fair hands, heart and head.

◆ **Boy oh buoyant.** Float You continues for as long as you are alive. Because there is always one more level of growth or challenge or success. As you keep loving it, your urge to learn even more increases. And the ability to keep learning and growing is the key to waking up each morning and saying boy oh buoyant it's great to be alive!!!

Give a damn

Activists are passionate. They make things happen. Imagine acting with that kind of fervour, the insistence and urgency – for the cause of you. Become passionate about what matters to you. I love … What exactly?

Write down five things, sunsets, people, foods, whatever – that really float your boat. Right now – things that really get to your heart.

I love:	because
1	
2	
3	
4	
5	

Activists are passionate. They make things happen. Imagine acting with that kind of fervour, the insistence and urgency – for the cause of you.

Shakespeare (paraphrased) said that the greatest hope would be to 'make the firstlings of your heart, the firstlings of your hand.' Passion is fuel for Float You.

At this point, where you really are ready to do the thing, it is really important to apply some safety checks. Think about how scuba divers take extra care to check instrumentation just before ascending to the bright light of surface. When it comes to instrumentation, please use your heart. It is a profoundly accurate measure. If you are about to float and the only one smiling at the prospect is you – be very, very cautious. 'I just want to get there, so I really haven't got time to give a damn.' If you can float in a way that shows you have breadth of compassion, chances are lots of people will want to keep you afloat.

◆ Give a damn – share your happiness with others.

◆ Give a damn – nurture relationships – be in the habit of applying your heart.

◆ Give a damn – consider your plan from the point of view of your close friends – is it good or bad for them?

Each time you don't give a damn, for example not returning an e-mail from a pal in a bit of trouble, you turn off your natural flow of human compassion. Which seems, from our evaluation, to be a major fuel source for whatever kind of goal. A love-free float will soon sink.

So now you know you have been through the float levels, quickly whizz out to wide-screen and see who is on the edges of your glory that could use a hand. Is there someone that has talked you through some of your early decisions, then you just lost touch? Pick up the phone. Have a pizza somewhere and say thank you. Now I really don't want to come over all Southern California but there is something very cool about being close to people. You get to a much better float feeling when it is genuinely shared. Random acts of beauty and senseless acts of kindness can really help.

Float You outcomes – as your personal power grows through float awareness you can apply some of your skills to a variety of situations. Have you thought about becoming a social crusader? No you don't get a cape with this one. But if you turn up at the local underfunded state nursery one Saturday morning with your team mates from the IT firm and transform the place, imagine how good you are going to feel. Get passionate about your life instead of someone else's profit. Being a good neighbour is (a) a nice way to live (b) potentially good for your businesss (c) allows you more chances to connect and open your heart. Plan to succeed with your heart as well as your head and hand. That's all.

Live large

Define your float hopes and dreams without limits.

Your imagination is yours. Success and happiness can appear on the screen of your thoughts in the most vivid way: music friends talking warm evening sunset images (one of Mick's!)

Your float dreams can come true with joy and ease. Expect it to be fun. Expect success. Not only in terms of how you make the most of your natural skills and talent, but also how you make the most of what the world out there wants to offer you.

The goal here is to find where you can optimize what the world offers and make the best of your natural skills.

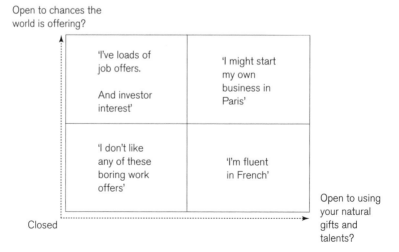

Open to chances the world is offering?

'I've loads of job offers.

And investor interest'

'I might start my own business in Paris'

'I don't like any of these boring work offers'

'I'm fluent in French'

Closed

Open to using your natural gifts and talents?

Are you open to success?

Start by identifying the live large offers being made to you right now by the world. By friends, employers, investors. By new markets opening up, new kinds of technology, by a new age. Then identify some of your own talents and skills. What are you good at? What do others tell you about your skills? Are you great with colours, good at listening, athletic, good with words? Consider those.

Now draw your own model using the above example and fill in the squares. Honestly. If you just can't be bothered, is it perhaps because you have lost sight of how good you are and how much the world might be trying to offer? All the float levels so far culminate in success only when you take a big breath and say 'I am open to succeed. I am ready to receive all the happiness I can possibly have, right here and right now.'

Ok, try it.

Expect success

Do you have large dreams? An image of what your success looks like? Live large is a mindset – your thoughts create your ideal life, your ideal work. Perhaps you find it hard to visualize yourself being really happy and successful. Work on this. If it is hard to even think happy, it will be even harder to live happy. Design the kind of life you want to live, think it so you can more easily achieve it.

Then live a little bit of that success every day. If your success means that you have more time for yourself, find an extra 2 per cent of the day that you have for yourself. Half-an-hour spent on your happiness. This investment, made regularly, will compound. As we said earlier, it is easier to act your way to a new way of thinking rather than think your way to a new way of acting.

Here is an example to help you try this out. First of all identify a few things that you do regularly. Then define the most incredible success that could grow from that. For example, if you are a musician, imagine the biggest gig of your life and how you would feel. If you look after people for a living imagine being able to reach out and make an even greater difference. If you work as an editor, imagine the whole industry worshipping you – reasonable given that you found and nurtured the best selling, most socially influential book ever!

Try.

Something I do regularly	The most successful outcome I can imagine. How do I feel?

Enjoy trying new things. Even if it's small. To live large is to float expansively. The most outrageous dress you ever wore to your firm's Christmas do, becomes brand you. (Especially when your name is Christopher and you work on reception.) Why not dress in your best clothes every day? What stops you sending a beautiful card today to someone you know would appreciate it? Live large in a realistic way, every day. Float You is a breakthrough in unlimited thinking.

You are designed for pleasure as well as duty. Can you handle that?

Martin's live large float

Remember Martin? He wanted to make a go of his job and get promoted within six months. He managed to work out his potential value to the firm, and he was quite a strong networker once he worked out it was about helping others as much as himself. Then he wrote a new palmPilot journal list – his Musp as he rather unfortunately calls it: Martin's Unique Selling Points.

He worked out that no one but him knew the inner workings of the old securities settlement system. Which was handy because a new project to upgrade it needed top people. He also knows everyone on the old system IT team because he used to play football with them. He also speaks Spanish and the new system is going to be piloted in Latin American territories.

Martin therefore has quite a few good reasons to be confident that he'll be on the candidate list for team New System S. If he does well on the project he is very likely to get the promotion plus 40k. And the rest, in terms of upward mobility, will be easy peasy.

There is one problem, however. He is not immediately noticeable. He is shy at meetings. His boss doesn't always remember to put him forward for new projects. There is a danger that he'll read about the new team rather than be in it.

Now live large is not about live loud. Because that is often one step away from live less long. Live large is unlimited thinking, openness to abundance. This is what happened to Martin when he turned on the live large programme.

'It was in the bath. I was lying there, completely knackered one Friday night and I figured it out. I was trying to be on the team. In a long line with lots of others. In fact I could pitch myself as the project manager – the team boss outright. No one at that level in the current organization has the knowledge I've got. And why not? They can only say no, and even if they do, it shows I've got guts.'

A mildly terrified Martin put forward a proposal to the senior team showing how the project could be kicked off three months ahead of plan. He described the risks and potential team members. He attached a brief biographical note entitled Your Project Manager, Martin Mears. Two weeks later, after a lot of discussion and a few beers, Martin was on a plane to Buenos Aires to brief the local pilot team. His live large approach had worked.

So here we are, and what about you? How is your live large strategy going? It doesn't need money. Live large in your thoughts first.

◆ Live large – create a bigger vision of your own success.

◆ Live large – teach people around you lessons in how to treat you well. They might want to, but don't know how to.

◆ Live large – take risks, know you can handle it if it doesn't work out.

◆ Live large – develop a level of comfort with more luxury (within your budget) than you are used to.

◆ How large? Are you comfortable with very? Because that is possible.

How to become rich

Let's define being rich as having a million dollars of net worth. To become a millionaire, according to Professors Richard McKenzie, of the University of California, Irvine, and Dwight Lee, University of Georgia, is almost a cakewalk. In their *Futurist* article (August/September, 1998) 'How Almost Anyone Can Become a Millionaire', McKenzie and Lee say, 'Most people in America got rich because they chose to do so, and they pursued a path to wealth that is wide open to most of the rest of us.' In other words, becoming rich is a matter of choice. Let's look at it.

Suppose a 22-year-old college graduate, earning $30,000 a year makes a one-time $2,000 investment in the stock market. With a 10 per cent compounded rate (which is the stock market appreciation over the last 50 years) that $2,000 would become $194,000 by the time he reached the age of 70. The person wouldn't be rich; but neither would he have sacrificed much. Suppose our 22-year-old was more serious about becoming rich and invested $2,000 each year. By the time he is 70, his wealth would exceed $2.1 million. Thus, the first step towards being a millionaire is to save consistently. In order to save consistently, you must avoid 'irresistible' temptations; make do with less expensive cars and clothing and cheaper entertainment.

Walter E. Williams December 14, 1998

(www.gmu.edu/depts/economics/wew)

Becoming rich later in life is a relatively small objective, if time and the principle of compound interest are allowed to do their thing. The live large challenge is to create a compelling financial future based on good, small steps here in the present.

Visualize large success before it happens. If we asked you, what would success look like in your life, you might say that it means the holiday of your dreams every year for the rest of your life. Or it might mean the keys in your hand to your dream home. Being able to see it is the first stage. Float You requires a strong belief in the likelihood of big change, big success, big happiness.

Ask the question

Float You helps you optimize your personal capital. But what if the float doesn't go well? Ask the question, do a worst case scenario. Asking better questions gives you better answers. You are going to float, and be fully prepared for whatever outcome, because you are able to ask the big questions.

Life is a pitch. By asking the right questions you validate your potential float and create a marketplace.

Ok, let's narrow this idea to one area. Say the field of sales. How might asking the right questions make a difference to the success of a salesperson? In the same way as the exercise above, asking the right question means asking open questions, and asking follow-up questions based on good listening skills.

Selling is about establishing a good rapport, trust and good quality information flow. The customer wants to feel relaxed and in control. The salesperson wants to gain specific information and build a good relationship in order to identify customer needs. Many salespeople fail to allow time in the process for customers to talk – instead they just go full on transmit. Which comes across as horribly pushy or unconfident or both.

The open, relaxed question can make a big difference. Ask the question. The FLOAT-question-based sales approach might help:

◆ **F**orward plan your strategy to gain entry. Planning produces performance.

◆ **L**isten to the customer. Identify real needs.

◆ **O**pen your questions! Use *what, when, where, who* and *how* to start the flow of conversation. Keep listening, responding.

◆ **A**ct on whatever selling signals emerge. If the customer wants to buy, make it easy.

◆ **T**rust build right the way through the sales process. Trust = good relationships = sustainable, ethical sales.

What about in practice. Might it work for one of our characters?

Lisa's questions

Lisa, as you'll remember, has been on a big float journey, travelling far from her original spot under the thumb of a pretty heavy boss. She now wants to bid to become the web master for a large insurance firm, based closed to her home. Lisa has now got four client accounts, which means that she has three freelance associates working with her, on a percentage of the rate charged to the client. Being the sole web provider to a firm this size would be a big breakthrough.

Her goal is to get the contract, hire the current web team as her own employees and improve their skills, so they can produce more interesting and innovative web designs. The firm gets more service at the same cost, and reduces employee costs. They have established that the in-house team are happy to transfer out – the benefits of new skills allowing better market mobility have persuaded them.

This is an important sales meeting. Lisa knows the stakes are high. And the IT director who she is due to meet is pretty stressed with lots of other demands on his time. Lisa prepares, sitting in the lobby downstairs.

Ok. The most important thing here is to stay calm. Remember there are plenty other fish in the sea. Not as big and lovely as this, maybe. I did my prep yesterday. Well at least I didn't leave it to today, with the boys being sick today I'd have had no chance. *(Forward planning)* Ok. What do I want to ask.

Remember my manners. First of all find out how he is. *(Listen)* Be on his side, if he is not able to talk because of some unforeseen meeting today, we can rearrange. How am I going to ask him – outright or subtle? I'll never know unless I ask him – ok 'would you like to go ahead with the contract discussed last week?' He might say no, he might say yes. Feels a bit high-risk – I'm driving back to the office ten minutes after he says no and that's that. Ok. Another question. 'What would outsourcing your web team to my company mean to you?' Better. *(Open question)* We can start talking and I know he thinks it will be a win win for everyone. Or 'what benefits would you expect from an outsourced web team, with added creative expertise?' 'That might work, but there's no way I can say that, it isn't me. Ok. I'll just ask questions that help him talk about the benefits and let him tell me how much he wants to make it happen. Then check he wants to sign and then say – 'when shall we get started then'. *(Act)* The most important thing is that even if he isn't ready to go for it now, he feels confident that I will respect his decision and still be on hand to help. *(Trust)* That's it. That's it. Right. Now where is the ladies?

What do you think? How is the meeting going to go? Will the outcome be a big new contract for our heroine? Is she about to live large? If she does, it's because she has faced her fears and asked the big questions.

Release the brake

Taking your foot off the brake is just as good as pressing hard on the gas. The brake is fear. So the float isn't likely to be here anytime soon unless you deal with your fear. As much as you need to put your foot down, moving your life towards the float, you also need to take your foot aff the brake and let go of failure. Stop being stopped by fear.

Let me explain that a bit more. What happens when you get into the car and put your foot down on the accelerator? You move forward. And what about when you put your foot on the brake. You stop the car. Fine. What about one foot on the brake and another on the accelerator, at the same time? Well, much shaking, shuddering, going forward and back and generally over-exerting everything. No forward motion but lots of exertion. Eventually the weakest link will snap.

This may sound familiar. Taking the brake off means identifying those things that you want to do – things that you are driving towards in your life – but which the brake of fear is keeping at a standstill. You want to, but are terrified. Shudder, creak. Bit forward, slam brakes. So you don't get anywhere. Although you use a lot of energy. 'I will write a list of people to talk to about my business idea. Just not today. I might follow it up and be rejected and that would be terrible. I'll just think some more about it. Talk to my friends again. Write another list. Go mad maybe.' Foot on the accelerator, foot on the brake.

Fear doesn't go away. In fact even the most experienced fight fear when they embark on a new venture. The point is it doesn't have to stop you moving forward. Gently try to take your foot off the brake.

The brakes in my life	What kind of thinking might take my foot off the brake?
Fear of looking stupid	What is the worst thing that can happen? It is much better to have a go and learn rather than wish and hope and keep my life stuck here.
I might try and they'll say no thank you. I am scared of being rejected	Even if I do get rejected, it doesn't matter. It won't kill me!

Add one of your brakes here	And foot off means?

And another

This Float You experience might be easier than you thought. Instead of foot down harder on the accelerator, you just need to ease off on the brakes. Easier, more do-able, cheaper. Feeling relieved yet?

So, returning to your float, 'Now float' focuses on a few key tactics. The goal here is to reduce your tolerance to failure, improve your sense of direction towards success. Write down what you most want to do. And what is stopping you. When you identify the brakes you can start to release them. Then the speed builds. Whatever you do is going to be better than just wondering if it might work. One line of thought is that there is no failure, just learning. Life would be a lot easier if we believed it.

Accelerator

Things you are doing – because they seem easy, but maybe not most important to you.	Things you really want to do, but are scared to try.
Things you can do, that are not scary – low priority.	Things you are mildly interested in, which are too scary to try anyway.

I want to do these – foot down on the accelerator

Brake

I'm scared to do these – foot down on the brake

Float You by taking your foot off the brake

The buck stops here

If it's to be, it's up to me

Play the hand you are dealt with and play it to win

Do it now. And most importantly, DO IT ANYWAY.

I learned that no matter who you are, where you come from, how you got that way and no matter what life throws full speed, you can respond, you can change and you can live the life of your dreams. To do so requires that we become responsible – 100% unconditionally responsible for doing whatever we must do to succeed.

Richard Bliss Brooke – profiled in New Entrepreneurs Ed Michael Ray and John Renesch

(Sterling Inc., 1991)

Love it

This is the essence of Float You. The feeling of inner success at finding a way to live and earn money while at the same time being true to yourself, living to your own values and sharing success with the people you love. Getting comfortable with yourself, allowing the good times to start rolling is also a way to overwrite the old negative programming we have all been raised with. So inner success creates sustainable outer success. We have talked about inside-outing – the sheer pleasure of knowing that you are happy in the moments when there isn't a team around to stroke your ego or a boss to say well done. The immensely refreshing calm that is constructed in the peaceful time you can spend in your own company. Listening. Not needing to be doing stuff all the time because you hate being alone.

Love it because there is a joyous way to live. What you have been doing through the stages of this book is creating self-belief, testing new skills, allowing new creativity. These gains compound into the floatable you. The person who knows about his or her personal capital and can take it joyously to market. That is an important little word snuck in there. If all we have done is help you create a successful, confident but joyless person, we've failed. Float now is float now with a sense of spirit and heart and joy – alongside all the market-facing skills and knowledge.

Ask any post-float individual how their life is going. This is the answer you'll get. I love it. Love it, see, taste, feel the pleasures of achievement, of being up there on a stage built with your own fair hands heart and head. So here is another checklist.

your float strategy

float you

momentum

Am I choosing a float that I love?

Write down the aspects of your life that you find most rewarding, spiritually recharging, fun.

1

2

3

4

5

Now write down the most satisfying experiences you have had so far in your working life, or in your studies.

1

2

3

4

5

Now let's consider your chosen float. In the next year, what do you anticipate as being the most exciting, satisfying, rewarding events as part of your float journey? Write your hopes here.

Now for a bit of application. What we want to do is to assess your float against the things that you know make you happy and satisfied and energized.

The love it or don't bother model

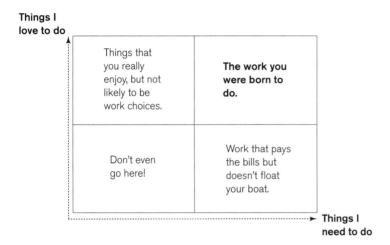

Things I love to do

| Things that you really enjoy, but not likely to be work choices. | **The work you were born to do.** |
| Don't even go here! | Work that pays the bills but doesn't float your boat. |

Things I need to do

Using the list you made earlier, draw up a chart like the one above filling in the boxes to assess the work that will really Float You. You want to float in a way that honours and rewards your spirit as well as your bank balance. So if your current float plans are not in the top right-hand box, consider if your current float plans are really right on every level. If they are a compromise or a stepping stone to get you towards the work you want to do, fine. Just keep moving towards the best you can have. Because you will get there.

Boy oh buoyant

Float You continues for as long as you are alive. Because there is always one more level of growth or challenge or success. As you keep loving it, your urge to learn even more increases. And the ability to keep learning and growing is the key to waking up each morning and saying, boy oh buoyant it's great to be alive!!!

Sustaining and growing Float You is another way of describing the rest of your life.

The lessons you have learned in each of the five float levels will continue to be learnt and applied to grow your confidence in a whole range of new situations. So buoyancy requires re-application of the float principles until they are a natural part of you.

This is an ongoing process. So when you hit your first big float goal – say you get the promotion you wanted – it is important to check again and find out where you are on the heart, head, hand power balance. If you are ruled by one or even two of these, rather than all three, your future float attempts will be out of balance. Heart, head and hand are, like a three-legged chair, best able to support you when all three are in balance and equal. The only one who can do that kind of check is you. So staying boy oh buoyant means balancing yourself, not hoping someone out there will take care of it. Success is inside out not outside in. Balance is inside out not outside in. How do you think you will be able to check this? Consider a quick review of one of your typical days. We know there is no such thing in your unique and busy life, but just try to identify what you actually do on a regular basis, what goes through your mind and how you feel. Hand, head, heart in that last sentence, in that order. Gut feel – is your life all about doing it and not feeling anything?

Or being highly emotional and not thinking things through? Or any combination?

A balanced float will be:

- making things happen, with feeling and awareness
- living mindfully, with your heart open
- expressing your thoughts and feelings through action.

Not sure which one of those works best for you? Try all three – is it an accurate representation of how you live your life? Check it out.

As each new challenge presents itself, there will be a buoyancy aid right here in the five float levels. And as you progress and succeed, being joyful, successful, abundant and unafraid will increasingly be a natural attribute of being yourself.

The best way to be happy is to decide here and now to be happy. The best way to be successful is to decide here and now to be successful. You have all you need to succeed right here and now in the present moment. That's why this chapter is called Now Float. Gently take responsibility for your own unique IPO. Decide to believe in yourself. Work out your 2 per cent change to take you closer to your float goal. Commit to it and stay with it. This will lead you to ownership of your own life and your own personal capital. It is yours to claim. That's about it for now. By all means check Float You.com to find out the latest on our Float journeys. There are more tools on the website to help and encourage you on yours.

staying afloat

float proposal

Your float will lead to a proposal, asking someone else for support. This might be your partner, boyfriend, bank manager, neighbour or any other stakeholder. The real test is to ensure that you are prepared for this meeting and can deal with any questions or issues that are raised by the other people.

We would never advocate that the five float levels are the answer to all your problems, but in our experience, if you can demonstrate control over the 30 key areas shown below then you have created significant advantage for yourself. You will have demonstrated that you understand yourself, value, network and market and how to make it happen. We believe that having such a clear view of your float will engender support wherever you go.

Know yourself

Choose your choice
Regain and retain the freedom to
make choices.

Know where you're going
Define the outcomes not the journey.

Map your map
Take decisions based on fact not fantasy.

Change how you change
Ensure all levels of your change are aligned.

Step inside out
Walk in the shoes of those people who are part of your float.

Share success
Always seek shared rather than selfish outcomes.

Know your value

Vote value not price
Value must always drive the price.

Powered by personal capital
Map and manage your personal capital stock and currency.

Dig deeper
Optimize your value by segmenting into the six primary levels.

Audit your assets
Determine the strength of your current assets against the capability required to undertake the float.

Benchmark your value
Ensure that the value you place on the float is realistic in the market.

Position your value
Be clear if you are offering your value as a commodity or niche product.

Know your network

Activate your abundance
Ensure you operate in synergy with your network.

Build a bridge
Reduce the inactive relationships and increase the interactive ones.

Chart the connections
Measure the level of clones and synergy to understand the value of your social capital.

Dare to be different
Ensure your network understand your proposition against that offered by other members of the network.

Entrust each other
Ensure that the people in your network will not erode your brand through poor promotion.

Fuel the flow
Take all precautions to ensure your
network doesn't decay over time.

Know your market

Sell the sizzle
Know how to sell the factors that
wrap your float.

Burn your brand
Ensure others never forget you or
your float.

Map the market
Make sure your float out-performs
any market shift.

Niche your niche
Target a market that is so specialized
that you can own it before others get
the chance to enter

Hit the hot spot
Use the tools of socialization and
specialization to get yourself to
market.

Market with meaning
Be real to yourself and your float in
your marketing.

Now float

Give a damm
Plan to succeed with a social
objective.

Live large
Define your hopes and dreams
without limits.

Ask the question
Always be prepared to ask people to
buy your float.

Release the brake
Before you put your energy into
moving forward, take your foot off
the inhibitors.

Love it
If you don't enjoy it then don't do it.

Boy oh buoyant
Once you have started – keep on
going.

staying afloat

float you

momentum

and finally ...

Parable

An investment banker was at the pier of a coastal village when a small boat with just one fisher docked. Inside the boat was a catch of several large yellow-fin tuna. The investment banker complimented the fisher on his catch and asked how long it took to catch them. 'Only a little while,' replied the fisher. The banker asked why he did not stay out longer and catch more fish, and the fisher said he had enough to support his family's immediate needs. The banker asked, 'But what do you do with the rest of your time?' The fisher said, 'I sleep late, fish a little, play with my children, take a siesta with my wife, and stroll into the village each evening where I sip wine and play my guitar with my friends. I have a full and busy life.' The banker scoffed: 'You should spend more time fishing and, with the proceeds, buy a bigger boat. With the proceeds from the bigger boat you could buy several boats. Eventually you would have a fleet of fishing boats. Instead of selling your catch to a middleman you would sell directly to the processor, eventually opening your own cannery. You could leave this little coastal village and move to New York where you will run your expanding enterprise.' The fisher asked, 'But how long will this all take?' The banker replied, '15 to 20 years.' 'But what then?' the fisher asked. The banker laughed and said, 'That's the best part. When the time is right you would float your company on the market and sell your stock to the public and become very rich. You would make millions.' 'Millions ... then what?' 'Then,' the banker said, 'you could retire, move to a small coastal village, where you could sleep late, fish a little, play with your children, take a siesta with your wife, and stroll into the village each evening, where you could sip wine and play your guitar with your friends.'

adapted from Doreen Lankshear-Smith 'Voluntary Simplicity'
(www.escape-ca/~mclachla/eyeopener/june00/junepage3.html)

We just wanted to make the point that float is just an analogy for fulfilment. Not just money.

Goodbye and good luck.

Carmel and Mick.

reading list

Level 1 Know yourself

◆ *The Seven Habits of Highly Effective People* – Stephen R Covey

◆ *Lead Yourself* – Mick Cope

◆ *The Fifth Discipline* – Peter M Senge

◆ *The Individualized Corporation* – Sumantra Ghoshal and Christopher Bartlett

Level 2 Know your value

◆ *Intellectual Capital* – John Roos, Goran Roos, Leif Edvinsson and Nicola Dragonetti

◆ *Know Your Value? Value What You Know* – Mick Cope

◆ *Creating Money* – Sanyo Roman

◆ *Think and Grow Rich* – Napoleon Hill

◆ *Competitive Advantage of Nations* – Michael Porter

◆ *The Ownership Principle* – Jeff Gates

Level 3 Know your network

◆ *Powerful Networking* – John Locket

◆ *Clicking* – Faith Popcorn

Level 4 Know your market

- *The New Marketing Manifesto* – John Grant
- *Business as Unusual* – Anita Roddick
- *Future Wealth* – Davis and Meyer

Level 5 Now float

- *Feel the Fear and Do it Anyway* – Dr Susan Jeffers
- *Follow Your Heart* – Andrew Matthews
- *The Activist's Handbook* – Randy Shaw
- *The Work you were Born to Do* – Nick Williams
- *Built to Last* – Collins and Porras